Writing for
the
Soaps

Writing for the Soaps

by Jean Rouverol

Writer's Digest Books

Cincinnati, Ohio

Library of Congress Cataloging in Publication Data
Rouverol, Jean
    Writing for the soaps.

    Bibliography: p.
    Includes index.
    1. Soap operas—Authorship. I. Title.
PN1992.8.S4R636   1984   808.2'2   84-17410
ISBN 0-89879-146-4

Design by Joan Ann Jacobus

To Mike, Susie, Mary,
Emily, Debbie and Becky,
who taught me that
life is soap opera.

The lyf so short, the craft so long to lerne,
Th' assay so hard, so sharp the conquering.

Geoffrey Chaucer

"The Parlement of Foules"

Acknowledgments

The quotation from Dorothy Parker in Chapter Six is from an article that appeared originally in the May 1936 issue of the *Screen Guild Magazine,* and reprinted in the WGAW anniversary issue of the *Newsletter.* Copyright © 1983, Writers Guild of America, West, April 1983, *Newsletter;* Copyright © 1936, Screen Writers Guild, Inc., May issue, *Screen Guild Magazine.* Reprinted by permissions.

I am also indebted to the Writers Guild West for permission to reprint their list of literary agents; and to Allen Rivkin, Elihu Winer, and David Davidson for the reference sources reprinted from the Writers Guild Newsletters both West and East.

And thanks to Harding Lemay for letting me use extensive quotes from his *Eight Years in Another World,* copyright © 1981 by Harding Lemay. Reprinted with the permission of Atheneum Publishers, Inc.

I am also indebted to Erik Barnouw not only for quotations but for many of his insights into the development of radio and television, as contained in his *A Tower in Babel,* copyright © Erik Barnouw and reprinted with the permission of Oxford University Press.

And thanks to the Harvard University Press for their decision that my use of the quotes from Gilbert Murray's *The Classical Tradition in Poetry* constitutes "fair use," thus simplifying everything!

The excerpt from Philip Barry's *The Philadelphia Story* was reprinted with the permission of Philip Barry and Ellen S. Barry. *The Philadelphia Story* copyright © 1939, 1940, 1942 by Philip Barry and Ellen S. Barry, copyright © 1939 by Dodd, Mead & Co., Inc., copyright © 1966, 1967, 1969 by Ellen S. Barry.

For the outline and script excerpt from *As the World Turns* I am indebted to Procter and Gamble Productions, Inc.: the material is reprinted with their permission, and the permission of the headwriters of the show at that time, Bridget and Jerome Dobson. Copyright © 1982, Procter & Gamble Productions, Inc.

For the outline and script excerpt from *Capitol,* I am indebted to John Conboy Productions, and to headwriter Peggy O'Shea and writer Craig Carlson; copyright © 1984 John Conboy Productions.

Excerpts of outlines and scripts from *Ryan's Hope* are used in this book by permission of American Broadcasting Companies, Inc., which is not responsible for its content. Excerpts from episode #2165, copyright © 1983, American Broadcasting Companies, Inc., and episode #2241, copyright © 1984, American Broadcasting Companies, Inc. I also want to thank headwriters Claire Labine, Mary Ryan Munisteri, and Paul AVila Mayer and writer Nancy Ford for their permission for my reuse of their work on the first episode, and thanks to headwriter Patricia Falken Smith and writer B.K.

Perlman for letting me excerpt their material in the second episode.

For the quotes from E.M. Forster's *Aspects of the Novel,* I am indebted to Harcourt Brace Jovanovich, Inc. Copyright © 1927 by Harcourt Brace and Co., Inc.; and © copyright 1954 by E.M. Forster; reprinted by permission of the publisher.

And finally, the ratings of the Daytime shows in this appendix are excerpted, by permission, from the A.C. Nielsen Index.

And then there are all the writers, actors, and production people to whom I am indebted for interviews, criticism, information and advice. For interviews written or verbal, my profoundest thanks to Agnes Nixon, Bridget and Jerome Dobson, Margaret DePriest, Ann Marcus, Wisner Washam, Edith Sommer, and Gabrielle Upton. For letting me excerpt from their writing, thanks to Nancy Ford, Claire Labine, Paul Avila Mayer, Mary Munisteri, Patricia Falken Smith, B.K. Perlman, Peggy O'Shea, Craig Carlson, Bridget and Jerome Dobson, Harding Lemay, Erik Barnouw; and for letting me reprint material they compiled and edited, thanks to Allen Rivkin, Elihu Winer, and David Davidson. For letting me pick their brains, thanks to Jack Herzberg, Robert and Phyllis White, Paul and Margaret Schneider, Theodore Apstein, Robert Soderberg, True Boardman, Linda Myles, Norma Connelly, Frances Reid, K.T. Stevens, Ray Goldstone, Rocci Chatfield, Glenhall Taylor, Manya Starr, Lenore Kingston Jensen, Amy Berkowitz and Hal Bowers, Jeff Corey, and Isadore Miller. For helping me with choices of material and clearances, thanks to Joseph Hardy, Mark Weston, Betty Wysor, Richard E. Shields, K.L. Fitz, William Behanna. Much gratitude to my editor, Barbara O'Brien. And many thanks to Naomi Gurian and the staff of Writers Guild of America, West, for providing me with material from their files which may prove useful to the readers of this book.

Contents

Writing for the Soaps

Preface

Someone—and my *Bartlett's Familiar Quotations* doesn't tell me who—said, "Freedom is the recognition of necessity." For the writer new to Daytime Drama, it is essential to understand the economic framework within which one's material is written, produced, and aired—or one can break one's heart and spirit fighting the restrictions. Once the boundary lines are clearly defined and accepted, however, and the reasons for them understood, Daytime remains a rich and satisfying field for the writer.

For a lot of reasons.

I happen to be of the school that believes Daytime can, and should, be *better* than prime-time episodic television. It's the one genre that allows for steady development of character. Where else in the entertainment world (outside of novels of course) can we spend so much time following the fortunes of a family—sometimes over several generations? Observing its Cains and Abels, its conflicts, its failures and triumphs, its losses and self-renewals? Watching its efforts to adapt to a constantly changing society? Where else can we observe, over those same decades, the impact of one wild cancerous cell—the villain—on the social body it inhabits? And where else can we see a child grow to adolescence and adulthood and even middle age, developing, changing, surviving one way or another the thousand natural shocks that none of us can ever quite escape?

And talk about the sins of the fathers . . . !

On Daytime we have *time* to do all this, because we air 260 episodes a year. And we have an audience that cares.

From its earliest and most simplistic days, soap opera has been increasing steadily in sophistication, in subtlety, in social responsibility. It no longer considers itself merely a means of distracting busy housewives. It is now bringing new insights into the lives and behavior of its viewers, and the times in which they live.

It is important, however, to know how we reached this point. How *did* the early serials evolve into their present form? What limitations are placed on the writer by rigid budgets and tight production schedules? How did the present "fractionated" method of Daytime writing come to be? And how does the need to maintain maximum viewership affect what we see on the television screen? Whether you, the reader, are a beginning writer or one already established in another genre, or whether you're interested in soap opera as an economic entity or as a mirror of our times—or even if you are, simply, one of the twenty million daily viewers upon whom the whole structure depends—you will find in the following pages the answers to some of these questions.

1
Beginnings

A couple of years ago, working as an associate writer on *Guiding Light,* I needed to call the Coast Guard to find out how an air-sea search was conducted. (Two of our characters, Hope Bauer and Alan Spaulding, had gone down to the Caribbean in a small private plane, remember?) Getting the details would be no great problem; the Writers Guild *Newsletter* lists a full column of phone numbers to call for this sort of information. I dialed the number given; got a courteous gentleman on the other end; told him I was a Daytime writer, and asked about the search procedure, which he described to me. Then he asked, "What show is this for?"

"*Guiding Light,*" I told him.

"Oh," he said. "That's not one of the ones we watch."

So now you know what Coast Guard members do when they're waiting to be called out on a rescue. They watch soap operas.

A few months later, I bumped into Norma Connelly, an actress who had become a regular on *General Hospital.* She told me that she and several other members of the cast, including the extraordinarily popular Tony Geary ("Luke"), were just back from leading a couple of soap opera seminars in the East. Where? Harvard.

Harvard? Harvard University? The intellectual hub of America? In Boston, Mass., where the Lowells speak only to Cabots, etc.? *That* Harvard?

Yes—at the Hasty Pudding Club, she said. And fans had almost mobbed the place, some of them climbing the fire escape and trying to break in through the windows. The police had to be called to get the actors safely away afterward.

3

That's when I learned that students all over the United States were planning their classes around certain serials. And that's when I discovered that Daytime Drama, popular with housewives since time immemorial, was reaching new and surprising audiences.

The Trials of Little Nell

A fascination with serials, a need to know "what happens next," did not begin with Daytime television or even its predecessor, the radio serial. E. M. Forster hazards the guess that "Neanderthal man listened to stories, if one may judge by the shape of his skull." He evokes an image of "(t)he primitive audience . . . gaping round the campfire, fatigued with contending against the mammoth or the woolly rhinoceros, and only kept awake by suspense. What would happen next?"

Well, we needn't go back *that* far, to make the point. We do know that Laurence Sterne, in the 1760s, published *Tristram Shandy* over a period of seven years—which must have nearly driven his readers up the wall. And we know that Dickens published all of his novels serially. In fact his serialization of *The Old Curiosity Shop* had built his audience to such a pitch (on both sides of the Atlantic) that the boat bringing the latest installment to New York was met at the dock by crowds shouting to the astonished crew to ask if Little Nell had died.

And there were others: Trollope, Thackeray (including *Vanity Fair*), Henry James—and even Harriet Beecher Stowe, whose *Uncle Tom's Cabin* had been contracted to run in the abolitionist *National Era* for three issues but which was still going strong nine months later. In France the form was called a *roman feuilleton*; Balzac and Dumas published serially from the late 1830s, with Dumas often writing episodes for several novels at once.

And so it went. American publications continued to carry novels of lesser quality but purpler prose for the rest of the century and into this one. We won't go into those lesser contenders however, nor will we get into a discussion of that other form of the continued story, the comic strip; it's enough to say that readers for generations—centuries—have found continued stories, in whatever form, irresistible.

Then, in the early part of the twentieth century, a new kind of medium came into being, the motion picture. It developed rapidly, and well before the outbreak of World War I, one-reel cliff-hangers were playing weekly at the local movie palaces, making Pearl White a household name. The craze endured for a couple of decades. There are staid senior citizens now for whom, as children in the 1920s, life would have been insupportable if they hadn't been able to catch the next episode of their favorite serial at the Saturday matinee—along with every other kid in the neighborhood. Movie serials were as much a part of the culture then as video games are today.

By the late 1920s radio was also becoming a national institution; and radio serials were a logical development. During the Depression the cost of a movie ticket kept a lot of people home listening to the radio instead. So a need for programming developed.

A few weekly thrillers had already begun to fill the vacuum. These were not serials as we know them, but nighttime weekly series of self-contained episodes like 1929's *True Detective Mysteries,* or *The Adventures of Sherlock Holmes* with William Gillette. *Amos 'n Andy* also made its appearance in 1929, and within a short time was reaching, it is estimated, half the families in the country who owned radios. Then came *The Goldbergs,* for the first time bringing a glimpse of ordinary (if ethnic) domestic life to the airways. *Clara, Lu 'n Em* also began chatting their way improvisationally through their evening time slot. The audience for these shows was expanding rapidly, and—perhaps most significant of all—sponsors like Colgate and General Mills were getting into the act.

And Now a Word . . .

Let's pause for a minute and consider the role of advertisers in the development of early radio. A show without a sponsor was called "sustaining"—meaning that the station or network had to sustain it. A sustainer was in much the same position as a Renaissance artist who didn't have a Florentine prince to support him; things could get very cold and hungry out there. We can't carry the parallel too far; Florentine princes weren't trying to sell toothpaste or cake flour, after all. But advertisers of the '20s and '30s, like their more patrician brethren, helped get the show on the road and keep it there.

During this period a couple of experiments were taking place in Chicago. Irna Phillips, a former schoolteacher turned actress-writer, tried her hand at a Daytime radio serial for women called *Painted Dreams.* It was broadcast only locally and didn't do well. At the same time an ad agency man named Frank Hummert, impressed by the popular success of serialized stories in newspapers and magazines, was also trying to develop the form for Daytime radio. His production, *The Stolen Husband,* written by Robert Andrews, was a failure, too, but Hummert was not discouraged, nor were the powers at NBC who decided to try *Clara, Lu 'n Em* as a daytime regular. That one, however, seemed to catch on. *Vic and Sade* came next, and then *Betty and Bob* and *Just Plain Bill*—all mild, leisurely, unsuspenseful pieces of Americana, not yet soap operas as we know them, but getting warmer. The year was 1932.

The following year, CBS introduced to its radio audience the first program that met all the now traditional requirements of true soap opera: *The Romance of Helen Trent*. Helen had it all—she was an embattled woman alone, with a special problem (she was thirty-five!), involved in every variety of melodrama, and with men appearing *seriatim* in her life. Her success encouraged the presentation of NBC's *Ma Perkins* with Procter & Gamble as sponsors. Daytime Drama was finally off and running.

By the way, it was the sponsorship of such household cleansers that earned early radio serials their sobriquet of soap opera.

The Soap Factory

By the mid-'30s another important event in the development of Daytime serials had taken place, not necessarily good in terms of quality, but a fact of life. Of the seven sponsored Daytime serials on the air in 1935, Frank Hummert and his wife Anne were responsible for five—clearly an impossibility if the Hummerts tried to write them all themselves. Their solution was to write an outline for each show, hand it over to a "dialoguer" to flesh it out into drama, let a supervisor do preliminary editing, and do the final editing themselves. Before the end of the decade they had a factory of about twenty writers working under them, half-a-dozen editors, and an army of secretaries.

Irna Phillips, who after her initial failure had found the requisite formula, now faced the same problem. She was simultaneously churning out *Right to Happiness, Woman in White, Road of Life, Guiding Light* (yes, as a radio show first, the story of four ministers), and *Lonely Women*. On only one or two of these was a collaborator listed; not until later was it revealed that she had been using a group of uncredited assistants. (I'll get to the plight of these anonymous drones in another chapter.) The assembly-line system she and the Hummerts evolved would project itself into the future, creating the current fractionated method of TV serial writing, and making "associate writing" a career itself.

On the other hand, Elaine Carrington, a writer of plays and magazine fiction who emerged in the 1930s as the creator-writer of *Pepper Young's Family, Rosemary,* and *When a Girl Marries,* did in fact do all her own writing. And managed, according to the critical consensus, to maintain a remarkable level of excellence in her shows. You pays your money and you takes your choice.

By the mid-'40s radio serials were flourishing. Their ratings dipped only slightly during the early days of World War II, and a number of new shows died a-borning, but in most cases strong story lines (often war-related) kept the audience of the more popular shows intact. Take 1945 as an example. Long-running serials included *The Romance of Helen Trent, Just Plain Bill, Ma Perkins, Backstage Wife, Big Sister, Pepper Young's Family, David Harum, Guiding Light, Bachelor's Children, Our Gal Sunday* ("... Can this girl from a little mining town in the West find happiness as the wife of a wealthy and titled Englishman?"), *Lorenzo Jones, The Road of Life, Woman in White, Joyce Jordan, Girl Interne, Valiant Lady, Young Widder Brown, Stella Dallas, Life Can Be Beautiful* ("An inspiring message of faith drawn from life . . ."), *Young Dr. Malone, Amanda of Honeymoon Hill*, the biblical *Light of the World, Portia Faces Life, The Second Mrs. Burton, Second Husband,* and so on and on. *One Man's Family* (". . . dedicated to the mothers and fathers of the younger generation and to their bewildering offspring . . .") had not yet moved to daytime from its longtime early evening spot, but otherwise the show met every qualification for soap opera.

Airways resonated with renditions (mostly organ) of signature music: "Red River Valley," "Juanita," "Stay As Sweet As You Are," "Sunbonnet Sue," "Valse Bluette," "Funiculi, Funicula," the theme from Tchaikovsky's *Pathetique,* "Estrellita," and "The Sheik of Araby" (otherwise known as "Destiny Waltz"), among many. During the next couple of years the number of serials settled down to a daily average of thirty-three.

Meanwhile, a new technology was developing in the wings. But to this writer (then an actress on one of the above-mentioned soaps) and to countless others, there didn't appear to be any cause for concern. Why should there be? Radio serials were enjoying a golden age, while television seemed little more than a new toy, and a faulty and experimental one at that. It was certainly nothing to worry about.

How wrong can one be?

Requiem for Radio

"Think, when we talk of horses, that you see them,
Printing their proud hoofs i' the receiving earth,
For 'tis your thoughts that now must deck
   our kings . . ."

(Prologue, *Henry V*)

7

Part of the One Man's Family *cast in Santa Claus Lane Parade, circa 1947, including Page Gillman, the author, and Susan and Mary Butler. NBC photo by Herb Ball.*

That, in a way, was radio. The listener was forced to flesh out the spoken word with imagination, becoming a co-creator with the broadcast personnel. The very completeness of television, giving us both words and image, deprives the audience of its ability to contribute, to be creative; whereas anyone who ever followed a radio show developed an instant image of what each character looked like. (One little old lady, to Michael Raffeto who played the dashing Paul on *One Man's Family:* "But your voice sounds *taller!*") This was the kind of creativity Thornton Wilder tried to evoke when he gave us *Our Town* on a bare stage: he wanted *us* to visualize the town, the streets, the houses. And we did, deriving extraordinary satisfaction from it. There's no doubt that in technology's gallop forward something has been lost.

And the world of radio was *fun,* in a way television can never be. Writers could pull the pages out of their typewriters and send them off to the continuity department without running the gauntlet, as TV writers do now, of heartbreaking rewrites by story editors or other writers who often turn the original material into something unrecognizable. Actors could arrive at the studio, pick up their mimeo'd scripts, read through them ("woodshedding" them briefly if there were a difficult scene or a foreign accent to cope with), do one rehearsal at the mike, and be ready to go on the air—playing word games with their fellow actors during commercials. There was an all-pervasive feeling of enjoyment and fraternity. Small wonder that a number of radio people, as radio drama disappeared, formed organizations like Pacific Pioneer Broadcasters, in which the pleasant, uncompetitive relationships of radio could be preserved and where monthly meetings still strive for a nostalgic reliving of The Good Old Days.

The last few years have seen a few attempts at reviving radio drama—but they have been anthology shows and mysteries, not serials; and their audience is small, their survival tenuous. A group called National Radio Theater did manage, with the help of some stunning actors and a grant from the National Endowment for the Humanities, to make an exciting mini-series out of Homer's *Odyssey.* However, mini-series do not exactly qualify as serials, not being open-ended. And anyway, let's face it, Homer's output was, well, finite. So he can't really be called a headwriter in the (you'll excuse the word) classical sense. Not like the Hummerts, I'm afraid.

The truth is you can't go home again. Commercial television serials may now be facing the first stirrings of competition from pay TV and cable—but the medium itself is here to stay.

Long Live the King

The first attempt at a Daytime TV serial was the unsponsored (and unsuccessful) *A Woman To Remember* in 1947. Not until four years later would a sponsor, Procter & Gamble, test the waters with another, the short-lived *The First Hundred Years.* 1951 would still prove a banner year for the television serial, however, as CBS introduced Roy Winsor's *Search for Tomorrow* (with Mary Stuart, then as now, playing the leading role) and *Love of Life.*

Considering that one episode of a TV serial cost up to two-and-a-half times as much as a radio episode in those early days, and that not many American families even *had* a TV set, one is astonished at the adventurousness of the sponsors of that period. For instance, *Ma Perkins* moved from a medium with the gratifyingly low cost of $164.56 per rating point (for a fifteen-minute show) to a vastly more difficult, complicated, and expensive medium with an audience no one could accurately predict. Looking back, one can't help being awed by such courage—or such prescience.

Production costs of fifteen-minute episodes in television did, however, prompt CBS to try to get more mileage out of its sets, actors, and crews. By the mid-'50s, two half-hour serials (*As the World Turns* and *The Edge of Night*) made their appearance, and audiences liked the new length. CBS in fact seemed to have developed a golden touch; while it was adding to its original two hits with four more between 1952 and 1956, NBC was fielding one show after another that couldn't quite make it.

A few radio shows tried to reach both markets at once. *Guiding Light,* after radical changes from its original radio format, flourished on television as well. *One Man's Family* didn't, though it continued as a popular radio show till almost the end of the '50s. By now, things were changing; more families owned TV sets, and by the second half of the decade, it was becoming increasingly clear that the TV serial was the wave of the future. A poll of *Guiding Light*'s audience indicated that the radio version was reaching between two and three million listeners, while the televised version was being watched in about three-and-a-half million homes, with considerably more effect as far as the sponsors were concerned. Perhaps it was time to contemplate a change.

Still, two or three million radio listeners were not an audience to dismiss lightly. And radio production was still enticingly cheap. What was it, finally, that tipped the scales and gave radio serials the *coup de grâce?*

Money, of course. Just as early advertisers had helped bring radio soaps into being, now a new and special financial consideration sounded their death knell. Local affiliate stations were finding they could sell advertising time to local merchandisers for more money than the fee they received for carrying network programming. In 1958 CBS Radio's affiliate stations demanded that the parent company give them more free time for local sales. Thus the networks could no longer guarantee an outlet for the national sponsors' advertisements. Naturally, the sponsors' interest in radio serials cooled. Early in 1959 CBS bowed to the new economic realities and killed four of its radio serials, including the still-popular *Our Gal Sunday. Helen Trent* met her end in 1960, followed in one black November week by four more long-running shows including *Ma Perkins, The Second Mrs. Burton,* and *The Right to Happiness. One Man's Family* had also just ended its extraordinary career on NBC. One by one, other radio shows gave up the ghost, while more and more television shows came into being. The king is dead, long live the king.

Beginnings

Shaping Today's Soaps

Those radio actors who had made the transition to television struggled to adapt. No longer able to read their parts script in hand, they now had to memorize them, often on only a few hours' notice, and perform them without benefit of the TelePrompTer, which was not yet in general use. Writers, too, coped with the new medium, wistfully remembering the infinite versatility of radio's sound men (storms at sea, crying babies, auto crashes, etc.) as they wrestled with the problems of a visual medium and the restrictions imposed on them by "live tape" production. In those troublous days, tape was edited (if at all) either manually or by a very primitive and not very dependable editing machine—a tedious process; and for that reason and reasons of cost, soap operas were shot all in one piece, without a stop. A director wouldn't interrupt a scene if the roof were falling in. "Establishing shots" were unheard of, and as for shooting on location—forget it.

The change from radio to television didn't faze Irna Phillips, however. She simply changed gears and kept on going. By the time of her death in 1973, she had created *Guiding Light, As the World Turns* (with Agnes Nixon), *Another World, Days of Our Lives,* and, from the Han Suyin novel, *Love Is a Many-Splendored Thing.* Nor had she lost her feistiness. When CBS got cold feet at the interracial story line of *Many-Splendored Thing* and demanded that she abandon it, she abandoned the show instead—to be justified soon after by the success of Agnes Nixon's highly ethnic *One Life to Live.*

This brings us to the heir apparent. Along with televised Daytime serials, a remarkable new talent appeared. Agnes Eckhardt (later Nixon) had just come out of Northwestern University with a degree in speech. Desperate to avoid her father's business (he manufactured burial garments), she arranged for an interview with the formidable Ms. Phillips, who read aloud a playscript the young woman had brought with her—and hired her on the spot.

At first, the newcomer worked under Phillips as an associate writer, then collaborated with her on the creation of *As the World Turns.* She spent six years as the headwriter of *Guiding Light* and two more on *Another World.* She created and produced *One Life to Live* and *All My Children,* continuing as headwriter of this last show until recently (though for a number of years she shared this task with Wisner Washam). She found time to write a mini-series, *The Manions of America,* and also created *Loving,* a new Daytime Drama for ABC which is currently headwritten by Douglas Marland.

Even in the early days of her career, Agnes Nixon has been consist-

11

ently willing to tackle sensitive subjects. Her *One Life to Live* carried a strong storyline about the nature of race prejudice. She also carried on a five-month campaign, integral to the storyline, about the urgency of Pap tests, and an eight-month campaign on venereal disease. In addition, she has involved her characters in problems of mental health, child abuse (I'll discuss *Loving* in this regard at a later point), ecology, and a returning POW's difficulties in adjusting to civilian life. We will delve more extensively into the networks' attitudes toward controversial subjects later, but when critics accuse Daytime Drama of not being relevant, defenders can point with pride to Agnes Nixon's record.

Trouble in Paradise

There were others who made major contributions to the new genre. One of the earliest television serials, *Love of Life,* created by John Hess, was produced by Roy Winsor, who himself created *Search for Tomorrow* (another 1951 offering, and now the longest-running serial on television) and *The*

All My Children's Darnell Williams and Debbie Morgan as the star-crossed young lovers Jesse and Angie Hubbard, with their staunch friend Greg (Laurence Lau). ABC photo.

Secret Storm, which came to an end in 1974 after a twenty-year run. *Edge of Night* was created in 1956 by Irving Vendig but headwritten for many years by Henry Slesar. And in 1963, Frank and Doris Hursley created *General Hospital* for ABC, though the show's extraordinary popularity is a fairly recent phenomenon. By chance or design, NBC premiered *The Doctors* on exactly the same day. Both shows showed women as competent, professional doctors and nurses—a giant step away from Irna Phillips' precept that "marriage is a woman's finest career."

In 1966 Dan Curtis created *Dark Shadows,* distinguished for three reasons: it boasted screen star Joan Bennett, it was Daytime's only gothic, and its most popular character was described by a television historian as a "charismatic vampire." There were, of course, a number of also-rans which appeared during these two decades, but the shows mentioned were the ones with staying power.

By the late '60s and early '70s, there was trouble in paradise: too many Soaps. At one point during this period nineteen Daytime serials were on the air, and the competition among the three networks was fratricidal. Ratings plunged. Perhaps viewers were suffering from confusion at too much of a good thing. Or perhaps the fault lay with the network executives who, in their desperate race to outdo the competition, demanded hyped up, overly dramatic stories and lost sight—at least in Irna Phillips' opinion—of the human values that had made the shows popular in the first place. Producer Roy Winsor said of those years that his network demanded so much money be spent on sets that acting budgets had to be cut, and shows suffered accordingly. TV critic-historian Robert LaGuardia comments: "One striking feature of this period in the history of Daytime television serials is the absolute insensitivity on the part of many producers to what viewers really wanted to see."

Whatever the reason, those few years saw a rash of cancellations, including *Secret Storm* and *Love Is a Many-Splendored Thing.* In a later chapter we'll examine the factors that combine to kill off an old and popular show, and we'll explore the other side of the same coin: why a network goes to all the expense of planning and mounting a new show, only to abandon it in a year or two before it's had a chance to build.

Meanwhile let's look at the more durable of the new shows, and at some of the production changes that appeared in the '70s and '80s. William Bell, who for many years was a headwriter on *Days of Our Lives,* created *The Young and the Restless* in 1973. In 1975 Paul Avila Mayer and Claire Labine created *Ryan's Hope,* Daytime's only show about a working-class family (a distinction to be discussed later). *Texas* was born and died, *Capi-*

tol came into being and, as of this writing, thrives.

Several innovations distinguished the '70s. One was the expansion, beginning with *Another World,* of a number of half-hour shows to an hour—a change that won the viewers' approval. Many headwriters find the new length more challenging and more rewarding, though one of them complains, "It just means you have to take twice as much aspirin!" Today the only half-hour shows are *Search for Tomorrow, Ryan's Hope, Capitol, Edge of Night,* and *Loving.*

An equally important development of the period was a substantial budget increase for many shows, which along with a steady improvement in techniques for editing tape, allowed Daytime to look more and more like motion pictures. Shows no longer need to be shot in sequence; the editor can now insert establishing shots, location scenes, stock shots, dream sequences, and flashbacks at will. For the Daytime writer who had been chafing under the restrictions imposed by "live tape" production, it has been like being released from bondage.

We will, in a later chapter, examine the production problems writers must still take into account when writing for Daytime; we'll examine other external forces that govern what and how they write (like the impact of audience response, e.g., the Nielsen ratings and fan mail, on storylines). We'll also look into the curious, symbiotic relationship that comes to exist between actor and writer, so that writers find themselves writing directly to an actor's special style. But for the moment these matters can wait. Our most immediate concern is the script itself because that's where it all begins. How does a Daytime script come to be? Does it spring fully formed from its writer's brow—or if it is a collaborative effort, who contributes what? And how, step by step, does it reach the sound stage where it will be taped and, finally, aired? Writing for a soap opera is not like writing for any other medium; it is a most difficult and demanding process, and it is worthwhile to find out how it is done.

2
The Assembly Line

In the beginning, there was the long-range projection . . . No, that's not quite right; in the *very* beginning, when a show was just coming into being, there was the bible (with a small *b,* please). This, in effect, was the creator's (again, small c) first statement of what the show was going to be about, and it included the major characters and their backgrounds, most of the minor characters, the locale (Oakdale? Henderson? Springfield? Pine Valley?), story lines for the first year or two, a week of sample scripts, and, if the network decided to go ahead, a "created by" credit for the full life of the show, a consummation devoutly to be wished.

But the bible, however essential, is only written once, and we won't concern ourselves with it at this point, whereas long-range projections are written, depending on the show, every three, six, or twelve months. An ongoing and urgent part of the Daytime-writing process, they are the road map that tells everyone involved where the show is going; so that's where we'll start.

In the recent past, while production has been continuing on the basis of previous story lines, a new long-range projection is begun by the headwriter after several days of intensive, exhausting conferences with the show's producer, sponsor, network representative, and sometimes representatives of the advertising agency. This projection runs anywhere from seventy to a hundred and fifty pages, detailing what's going to happen in the immediate future to each story line and each relationship. In the projection the headwriter makes clear when the major story is going to "peak" and come to a climax, and which of the secondary stories will then move to the foreground.

He also makes sure that all the story lines are interrelated to some degree. One network calls this "cross-wiring."

Some headwriters use the projection as a selling job to keep the sponsor happy. (Harding Lemay, in his autobiographical *Eight Years in Another World,* reports Irna Phillips' advice to him about his first long-range projection. "My main objective," she said, "should be to convince [the sponsors] that I knew what I was doing, not to tell them what it was.") Sometimes the headwriter will try to capture in his narrative, as a guide to the associate writers and the production team, some of the qualities he wants communicated in the shows themselves: warmth, comedy, suspense, or whatever else; so the projection is sometimes written like a novella.

(And here, an aside. The writer of a book must, in the interests of simplicity, make certain choices. Just as I have elected to describe, in these early pages, the writing of a one-hour show as opposed to one of a half-hour, I am also electing to use the conventional *he* when I refer to members of the writing team. Even though Daytime is the one area of the media which employs as many women writers as men, or even more, I'll stay with tradition and use the generic male pronoun. I trust my women readers will agree that using *he/she* throughout would be a syntactical nightmare.)

The One-Week Breakdown

Now the makers of the show have their roadmap and can go forward. At this point the headwriter breaks down the longer projection into one-week outlines or, almost too descriptively, "breakdowns." I will reproduce one of these documents in a later chapter; but in the meantime, let's examine what a breakdown consists of.

It is a brief (or not so brief) narrative of the week's developments, Monday through Friday; it assigns each day's segment to one of the associate writers, telling him what day the show will be taped, what day it will be aired, and most important of all, *what day the finished script must be in the headwriter's hands;* the headwriter must receive it *on time and in sequence* so he can correct it in its proper order (more of this later).

Each daily breakdown runs from seven to thirty pages, depending on how loose or tight a leash the headwriter keeps his associates on. The breakdown specifies where each scene of each act is laid, which characters appear in each scene, and what happens therein. Sometimes key lines of dialogue are included to give the essential tone and direction of the scene. If mood is important, the instructions will say so. And the Friday show will usually end on a "hook," leaving the viewers cliff-hanging so they'll be sure to tune in on Monday.

But before the breakdowns can even be sent to the associate writers, they have been rushed to the sponsor and producer, who call in their corrections to the headwriter. For this reason, some headwriters write their breakdowns with wide margins on either side, where these last-minute changes and amendments can be scribbled. To retype would be too time consuming, so the corrected pages are simply Xeroxed and sent off to the associates, usually by messenger or express mail. Running, running . . .

The associate writer, who usually knows when to expect his outlines, doesn't dare leave his house for fear of missing the mail and delaying starting his script by a day. With only a five- or six-day writing schedule for an hour show, a day lost would be a catastrophe. As a rule, the breakdowns are still warm from the mailman's hands when when the associate sits down to read them. He reads the whole week's outline once to get a sense of the story's thrust; then he rereads the breakdown just prior to his own to have firmly in mind the situations leading up to the scenes he must write. A few moments' thought (depending on whether he plans his scenes in his head, or on paper as he writes)—and then he gets straight to the typewriter to start turning his assigned seven- to thirty-page outline directly into seventy pages of drama.

Time Is Still A-flying

Learning to budget time is an essential part of writing for the Soaps. It is as important as learning to live within your income when you have a small salary and two mortgages. And it's not enough simply to divide the number of pages in a script by the number of days one has to write them. Few writers get every scene right the first try, and our associate writer would be wise to budget time for revisions (and other exigencies). Let's say he needs to cruise (for an hour show) at the rate of fifteen to seventeen pages a day unless he's one of those supermen who can write *two* shows a week; then double the above figure. A novelist would cringe at such a pace but the Daytime associate writer has no choice, and learns to do it. In fact, a Daytime writer almost never gets sick. He can't afford the time.

However, plenty of other emergencies arise to interrupt him. Sometimes the breakdown calls for a medical or courtroom scene, and the harried associate must carve time out of his day for a trip to the library. Or he must put in phone calls to doctors or lawyers to learn the proper procedure and terminology. He also has to make sure that the material he uses is not only accurate but colloquial; he can't allow his doctors to sound like pages from a medical encyclopedia—and doctors do have a surprising number of pet names for medical procedures. Also having done his research, he needs to pass on the information to his fellow associates, so their handling of the material will be consistent with his.

Which brings up another matter. Since the content of each show necessarily follows that of the day before, no associate writer dares to be too innovative; it throws the whole team off. Each scene may progress only to the point the headwriter has indicated in the breakdown and not a step far- ther. The associate understands that he is as much a part of a continuum as an automotive machinist fitting the doors on a car's chassis as it moves past him. His job is part of the *whole.*

Now, after writing the best show possible within the allotted five or six days (and if it's a P&G show, having appended a one- or two-page summary of the episode's developments) the associate clean types his script, and at- taches a title page containing the essential information about the episode (script number, taping and air dates, names of the members of the writing and production teams, each actor used in the cast that day, and each set, in- cluding flashbacks and dream sequences). Also, whether it's a new day or the same day as the preceding episode. He Xeroxes everything and sends it to the headwriter by the fastest method possible. (Every day spent in deliv- ery means one day less for writing.) And then, in the half day left before the arrival of the next set of breakdowns, he tries to take care of the thousand personal or domestic tasks that have been accumulating since *last* week.

How do you tell a Daytime writer from every other kind? He's the one who's always breathless.

Return for Rewrite

Now let's follow the associate's script back to the headwriter again. Since we left him, the headwriter has been editing (i.e., correcting) the previous week's scripts, and has written and mailed off another set of breakdowns. The new scripts, five of them, arrive almost simultaneously, and he begins at once to read and correct them—*in sequence.* Most headwriters hate to cor- rect scripts out of their proper order, and any associate writer who has not met his deadline is not likely to keep his job. The script-editing process will be analyzed in another chapter; right now it is enough to say that the headwriter makes sure each script conforms to its breakdown. He corrects dialogue to make it consistent with that of the preceding script (which was written by a different writer). The headwriter makes sure each associate has dealt consistently with each character. Finally he eliminates as far as possible stylistic differences among his various associates. How much actual rewriting is done depends on the particular headwriter: some rewrite only to correct character or sequential discrepancies; others rewrite almost compulsively because they have a private concept of each scene, and no one else's vision of it ever seems quite right.

One headwriter admits that many rewrites are simply a matter of personal taste. "It's like," she says, "choosing wallpaper."

Naturally the headwriter corrects any flaws in the dramatic thrust of the material. The week's five scripts must move the story forward and give it a *trajectory*.

Here it's necessary to interpose a thought: the sequence described above applies when a headwriter does his own editing. On some shows there is now a team of headwriters, and the editing is assigned to someone employed just for that purpose. Sometimes the job is broken up even further—one writer for the long-term story, another for the breakdowns, a third for editing. Increasingly, certain shows, including *General Hospital, All My Children,* and the Procter & Gamble shows use the team approach.

However, let's stick with our hypothetical do-it-all-oneself headwriter. After correcting the scripts to his satisfaction, he turns them over to his team of typists who type them in multiple. Several copies are sent to the sponsor, several to the producer, a couple are kept on file. However, our headwriter has already started the process all over again with *next* week's breakdowns and scripts. No rest for the weary.

As soon as the week's corrected scripts reach the production office, whether in Los Angeles (*General Hospital, The Young and the Restless, Days of Our Lives, Capitol*) or New York (all the rest of the Soaps), the producer reviews them carefully to make sure they follow breakdowns. He also corrects for length (some producers read scripts aloud and time them with a stop watch, indicating possible cuts); checks for backstory inaccuracies (if he's been with the show longer than the headwriter and hence more familiar with the characters' history); occasionally corrects language if it seems stiff or difficult for the actor to read; and makes sure there's nothing in the script to upset Standards and Practices. This office, by the way, exists at each of the networks; its function is to make sure there's no action or dialogue in any show, day or night, that would offend public taste or damage the network's public image.

The producer's corrected scripts are then passed on to an experienced production secretary who inserts technical and commercial cues, (turning the scripts into final shooting material before they are copied).

At this point the producer holds a production conference on next week's five scripts. Present are all the technical people: head electrician, head stagehand, heads of props and wardrobe, art director and his assistant, and production assistants. The producer discusses the general production aspects of the scripts. Prior to this, production assistants will have made a breakdown of each script—sets to be used, actors and props used on each set, and any special wardrobe problems. At the production meeting, the various department heads bring up any questions they have; the entire meeting should take a couple of hours.

By now the copied scripts have been apportioned to two or three directors. A few days prior to his shoot, each director meets the art director and discusses the set plan. The director settles down with his script to visualize the scenes. With the set plan at hand, he marks each camera cut on the script indicating a medium shot, medium long, close, or whatever it is; numbers it; and on the floor or set plan he will mark each camera position. (One director reports that he spends about seven hours per hour show on this process; that's probably a fair average.) Then he holds his own production meeting with the technical and lighting directors, giving the technical director (TD) an exact copy of the production script and discussing any possible problems. The technical director makes "shot sheets" for each camera, using the director's shot numbers for purposes of identification.

The actors should have received their weeks' scripts at least seven days in advance of taping, and they are now busy memorizing their parts. Some shows try to limit the use of actors to three shows a week; working more often than that makes life very hard for the actor. Other shows are less considerate. *The Young and the Restless,* for instance, seems to have no compunction about using its actors four or even five times a week. Can you imagine memorizing five one-hour scripts per week? Cue cards and Tele-PrompTers aren't always available. On Procter & Gamble shows, for instance, their use is frowned on; the official position is that these devices "destroy spontaneity," though actors suspect P&G's real objection is Tele-PrompTer's estimated $65,000 cost per year per show.

Time to Tape

And now, the taping.

The technicians—lighting, sets, props, and so forth—arrive at the studio well before daylight (2 A.M. is not uncommon). The director gets there early and may already be walking the sets as the actors arrive (any time from 6 A.M. to 8:30 A.M.)

The director and the actors then "block" the show, stepping out the movements, in one of the studio's rehearsal rooms. At this point, the actors still have their scripts in hand. Now the camera and sound crews arrive, and the director may have a brief discussion with them. Then—and it's still fairly early—there's a dry run for cast and crew; the cast, still with scripts in hand, walk through their movements as the cameras watch. (This rehearsal is also known as a "tech," short for technical.) Then there's a run-through for the actors, who by now have put their scripts aside. On *Days of Our Lives,* for example, these steps are combined with each scene rehearsed twice in succession, once for the cameras and once for the actors. Just before noon, there's a break for lunch and hairdressing or makeup if these necessary items haven't already been taken care of. (NOTE: Again, I am describing the routine on an hour show; a half-hour show is somewhat less grueling.) After lunch a dress rehearsal with costume and makeup is held. In this rehearsal the cast goes straight through the show without stopping for instructions. The producer and executive producer watch either from the control room or on a monitor, as they make notes.

By early afternoon, the producers' and director's notes are given to the actors. Timing or shading of scenes is corrected. If the stopwatch has shown the show to be too short or too long, a call goes out to the headwriter to ask for cuts or additional material, and these changes are given to the actors at this time.

Apart from such an emergency, no mention has been made of the writers during the production process. Why aren't they present on the set?

For two reasons. First, headwriters and associate writers are too busy at their typewriters to waste time in a situation where they really have no further function; they've already *done* their work. Second, directors tend to discourage contact between actors and writers. Just as directors know they make little or no story contribution, they also feel it's better for a show in rehearsal to have one source of authority—the director. A writer on the set adding *his* opinion about the scenes or characterizations would only serve to confuse. Even Agnes Nixon, who keeps a close eye on every aspect of her shows, chooses not to be present on the set often, for fear of blurring the lines of authority.

In addition, on certain shows—*General Hospital* is one, according to one of its actors—the producer follows a deliberate policy of never letting the actors know the long-range storyline in case they allow this knowledge to affect their performance. *Hospital's* Gloria Monty has said that since life is a surprise, it's better if the things that happen are a surprise for the actors

Together onscreen and off: Doug and Julie (William Hayes and Susan Seaforth Hayes) on Days of Our Lives. *NBC photo.*

too. It keeps them more on their toes.

So, in most cases, producing the show takes place in a world apart from that of the writer.

By now, depending on the show, it's 2 or 3 P.M. Time for taping.

For reasons of economy, shooting sequence is based on *sets;* as a rule, all scenes played in a given set are shot in one batch regardless of their order in the script. This may be hard on the actors, but it consolidates the work of the crew and keeps down production costs. One fortunate exception is *All My Children,* which shoots scenes in the order in which they occur in the script. Also for reasons of economy, reshooting a scene is rare—unlike those endless retakes on a movie set. In earlier days, when editing tape was a difficulty, reshooting was discouraged because it meant stopping and rolling the tape back to the start of the act and rolling again from there. Now, however, if a Daytime actor blows his lines, the company merely backs up to a point where they can make a good cut and starts that portion of the scene again. However, on any Daytime set, speed and economy are still the watchwords.

Between six and eight in the evening, often more than twelve hours from the time of the director's arrival at the studio, taping is finished, and the editor takes over.

Editing, again? Didn't the headwriter already edit the script? Yes, but there are two uses for the word. In this case we're referring to the "cutting" of the tape, or more accurately, the electronic splicing. Scenes shot out of sequence are joined together in sequence. If the script contains a dream sequence, a flashback from an earlier show, optical effects, or an exterior establishing shot, it is now added to the tape by an editor who is skilled in the use of the computerized electronic editing machine. Also appended are the show's opening signature, the commercials, and the closing credits. However, shows taped in the West are sent to New York to have the commercials added electronically. As a rule, very little sound editing is necessary; sound effects and music have been recorded live during taping. For an average show, the entire editing process should take about three hours.

But what if one segment of the company has been shooting on location in Greece or the Caribbean? Those scenes have been shipped back, and the editor finds himself with a much more exacting task: sorting amid the available material for the best shots. Also, it's likely some sound editing will be required since circumstances are rarely 100 percent controllable on location; sound effects will have to be added (this is called sweetening). Altogether, editing location sequences can add six or eight hours to an editor's job.

At this point, if the show was shot in Hollywood, it is shipped East; airing of all shows takes place there. To allow for time differences, however, the separate outlets in the mid-West and West record the New York broadcast and rebroadcast this new recording in their own time slot. The air date is usually about a week after the show's tape date.

The Rush of Adrenaline

How long, from the writing of the breakdown to the final airing, has the whole process taken?

It varies from show to show. Wisner Washam usually outlines *All My Children* seven weeks before airing. Bridget and Jerry Dobson (formerly of *General Hospital, Guiding Light, As the World Turns,* and currently creating their own *Santa Barbara* for NBC) like a spread of at least six weeks. If a headwriter ever wants a vacation, the only way he can achieve it is by accelerating the writing process by assigning an extra script or two per week until his stockpile of scripts has increased by the number of days he wants to take off.

However, one disadvantage of having more than a normal number of scripts on hand is the ever-present possibility of one of the actors getting sick—in which case, more finished scripts only means more rewriting.

Some headwriters work better under pressure ("I need the rush of adrenaline," says one), so they don't need or want much lead time. But during the Writers Guild strike in 1981, there was chaos. All of the shows were scab written, in most cases badly, and much lead time was lost. *As the World Turns,* for instance, lost five of its comfortable seven-week margin. And on another show, "We were writing dialogue off the bulletin board," says one company member—almost improvising, in other words. Walking the writers' picket line sounds peaceful by comparison.

Now that we know who supplies the component parts of a daytime drama, let's go on to examine the actual writing process in greater detail. Recognizing the extraordinary number of limitations placed on the creativity of every member of the writing team, it's important to know how they manage to function at all. Again, let's leapfrog the writing of the bible, and go directly to the headwriter of an established Soap and find out how he does his job.

3

The Not-So-Wingéd Muse

Robert Frost said that writing free verse is like playing tennis without a net. A new headwriter, taking over a show created by someone else, is literally surrounded by nets. He is a captive of the rules of the game and must quickly learn to operate within them.

Let's suppose that the current headwriter of a Soap is leaving his job and the company is looking for a replacement. They have interviewed the candidate—a playwright, perhaps, who's new to Daytime; and they've found his off-the-cuff comments about the show perceptive and his ideas interesting. So they've asked him to track the show for a few weeks and provided him with scripts and past story projections so he can further familiarize himself with the show's style and back story. He may or may not have been asked to write (for a sum, of course) a sample projection. (And please take note: these negotiations take place only with writers already established in Daytime or another writing field; *if a story projection arrives at the producer's office unsolicited, it will be returned unopened for fear of future plagiarism suits.*) In any event, on the basis of these conversations or the sample projection, the sponsors and/or other executives decide they like his general approach, advise him that he's hired, and ask him to come to his first long-range story conference.

Let's pause a moment for clarification. What's the relationship between the story conference and the writing of the projection? The answer depends on our headwriter's experience in soap opera. Certainly when he's taking over a show, the conference takes place *before* the material is committed to paper—his first, harsh lesson is that he is not autonomous. Story decisions must be shared by the network representative, the show's executive producer, and, on Procter & Gamble shows, by *their* representatives. Our new headwriter, recruited to this field from playwriting, may recoil at the prospect of so much involuntary collaboration. (Remember the old joke about a giraffe being a horse put together by a committee?)

However, if the writer's a veteran of prime-time television, he's already used to the group-think process; and if he's served an apprenticeship as an associate writer on this or another Daytime show, he knows what to expect.

On the other hand, if he's been the chief writer on this show for a period of time, or has built up a reputation as a solidly dependable headwriter on other shows, he has enough clout to work the process in reverse: he gets general approval on his plans, then writes the projection, and *then* has the conference based on the story lines in his projection.

Into the Lions' Den?

But let's assume that our headwriter is fresh to the job and on trial. He has to run the gauntlet of the story conference first. What's such a meeting like? Where does it take place? What's on his mind as he walks into that conference room?

In all likelihood, the conference is held at the network's or sponsor's office in New York, and if our newcomer is not a New Yorker he is flown there for the occasion. Or the sponsors and producer may travel to meet the writer in his hometown where they've taken a hotel suite. Or, if the writer is affluent and can accommodate all those executives at his home, *that's* where they'll meet. Whatever the setting, however, our headwriter probably goes into the meeting with mixed feelings. Even though he's new to soap opera, he undoubtedly feels qualified for the job by proven competence in branches of writing other than this one; he has, after all, been trained in dramatic writing and may feel he understands it better than a group of business executives. So he may be prepared for a fight.

Needlessly, in most cases.

Except in those rare instances in which a headwriter is either owner or co-owner of his show (e.g., Agnes Nixon, William Bell), the shows are owned by the network, the producer, or the sponsor (Procter & Gamble owns five). A successful soap opera is an extremely valuable commodity, and most executives who've been with it a long time have a vested interest in its welfare. Though a frustrated headwriter may feel the executive approach is more commercial than artistic, those people have been through a lot of ups and downs with the show, and have an accurate sense of what the audience does and doesn't like. So executive input may prove valuable.

Certainly their intentions are good. Jacqueline Smith, ABC vice-president in charge of Daytime programming, says: "Executives at ABC are there to support the creative impulses of its people." Wisner Washam of ABC's *All My Children* feels the conferences with his executives are highly productive. And Margaret De Priest, former writer of *Love of Life, Where the Heart Is, How to Survive a Marriage,* and, currently, *Days of Our Lives* says of working with Jacqueline Smith, "I learned a lot from her. She changed the viewing habits of a nation."

How about the sponsor-owned shows? Headwriters who have spent hundreds of hours in conference with Procter & Gamble's story executives Bob Short and Ed Trach give them high marks for intelligence, helpfulness, and constructiveness. (Trach is, in fact, a graduate of the Yale Drama School.) What are some first-hand reports? Edith Sommer, now busy writing plays, but who with her husband Robert Soderberg was headwriter for *Guiding Light, Search for Tomorrow,* and *As the World Turns* says of the P&G representatives, "They had an easy manner, great kindness and integrity." Ann Marcus, whose debut as headwriter was on *Love Is a Many-Splendored Thing* but who subsequently wrote a number of P&G shows (*Search for Tomorrow, Days of Our Lives, Love of Life*), says of conferences with Trach and Short, "I really enjoyed the give and take. There was a lot of respect, a lot of humor." Jerome and Bridget Dobson say much the same. "We respected the people we worked with."

There you are. In spite of all the misgivings one may have, the collaborative conference generally proves more of a help than a headache.

But before we get into the conference itself, let's mention a new situation that is evolving in the sponsor/network/producer structure. Increasingly, Procter & Gamble is turning over final authority on story decisions to executive producers in charge of the shows. Trach and Short are no longer so actively involved in story planning, and Short in fact left the corporation altogether last year. The net effect is that headwriters for P&G are losing their best friends at court and still more of their authority. The reaction is one of dismay. One former headwriter says, "We never owned our shows, but we were *always* in charge." And the Dobsons state the problem even more firmly. "Successful soaps have been created by passionate writers, *not* by passionate producers."

But the times, they are a-changing, and perhaps this shift in authority is taking place because of ABC's domination of the Daytime ratings race—exactly the years Jacqueline Smith has been in charge of the soaps

Getting to know you: Tom Nielsen and Lisa Brown as Floyd and Nola on Guiding Light. *CBS photo.*

at that network. Another possibility is the desire of other soaps to emulate the remarkable success of *General Hospital,* with the brilliant (and strong-minded) Gloria Monty as executive producer. Monty came to production from Daytime directing and has brought *Hospital* a razor-fine sense of pace and movement. If you want to know what it's like on that set, consider reports that say it's where the writer, director and star of *Tootsie* did their research.

Whatever the chain of command at the story conference, however, and whether or not a sponsor and ad agency are represented, the process itself is the same. The participants struggle through two long days and endless cups of coffee, analyzing, arguing, suggesting, and shooting down each other's suggestions, laughing when they're able to, and once in a while having a flash of inspiration. Decisions that a more experienced headwriter would be making alone at his typewriter are made jointly here—and some of the decisions are not easy.

. . . To Murder and Create

First of all, there's the matter of the characters and storylines our new headwriter inherits from his predecessor. Should they be kept or discarded?

That decision depends on how well the show is doing when our newcomer comes aboard. If the ratings are high and the preceding headwriter is leaving the show of his own accord, the new arrival is expected to maintain continuity and not rock the boat. But if the former headwriter has been fired because the fan mail is negative and the ratings are down, radical remedies are in order.

Apart from the "core" characters who are sacrosanct, there are many characters not created in the original bible who have been added to the show at various moments in the past to serve story purposes now long forgotten. Their survival is probably more of a tribute to the actors who play them than the writers who drafted them. Nevertheless, there they are and must be dealt with. Which of them should be kept, and which disposed of? If the decision is to dispose of some, the headwriter must then decide whether it's better to write them out or kill them off. If the show is doing very badly and the network, producer and sponsors are desperate, they may give in to the headwriter's understandable impatience and allow him to "send the car over the cliff"—to dispose summarily of a whole group of characters who stand in the way of new story lines. But our new headwriter and his fellow conferees must weigh the relative merits of dispatching these characters or moving them quietly into the background for unobtrusive trips to Denver or San Francisco during the next few months, making way gradually for new people and stories that may offer more conflict and excitement.

It's probably wiser to exercise patience and restraint in shifting from one set of story lines and characters to another. In addition to the "core family" who have been on the show from the outset, there is a core audience who probably have been watching for years; they identify those core characters with the show itself. "You don't altogether know what they're most devoted to," says Margaret De Priest, "so you build on what's there."

Actually, whether the show is doing well or poorly in its current state, it will take our newcomer a certain amount of time to work toward his particular concept of what the show ought to look like. The Dobsons say it takes about six months before they begin to feel "comfortable" with a show—before it begins to truly represent their own tastes, their own ideas. Ann Marcus (who in addition to her other credits also co-created *Mary Hartman, Mary Hartman,* thus turning the soap opera concept on its head) says she was unhappy with only one of the shows she took over; the rest, she felt, were in good shape. But she adds, "Each headwriter has a certain style and a unique quality, and wants to put his or her imprint on a show."

No matter how gradually or abruptly the transition is made, however, the existing story lines must be resolved in a dramatic and believable manner before the new stories are introduced.

What about those new stories? Our newcomer undoubtedly came into the story meeting with a number of ideas which have, since the meeting began, undergone a rich sea change. Some plans may have been vetoed because they too closely resembled situations on one of the network's (or sponsor's) other shows. Other plans may have been thought predictable and twisted into a different shape by the addition of new factors. And everyone at the meeting has come up with ways to interweave the various stories because—as our newcomer quickly learns—stories cannot run parallel only, they must carom against each other like billiard balls. What happens to characters A and B, he learns, *must* have an impact on characters C and D, and a catastrophic effect on E and F. The ripple effect even touches characters G and H. For a one-hour show, eight to ten story lines are needed—all interwoven. Each story line must be designed for growth; each must contain contradiction and conflict and must promise suspense. Again and again, each story line must resonate against the others. If our newcomer had neglected to remind himself, he has learned again during this two-day session that no man is an island—especially in Daytime Drama.

For most of the headwriters I've talked to, this requirement for a multiplicity of interconnected stories is as exciting as a fire alarm to a fire house dalmatian. "It's a wonderful test of logic," says Ann Marcus. "It's like moving the pieces in a chess game." As for the stories themselves, Edith Sommer says they are essentially evolutionary. "The characters grow and change," she says. "Events change character. Characters affect events." Another headwriter is equally unfazed: "Every story comes out of another."

The meeting goes on until a consensus about the show's direction for the next four, six, or nine months is reached; and the headwriter—by now altogether exhausted—staggers home to turn his notes into narrative in the form of the long-range projection.

Modus Operandi

At least that's the procedure on many shows, but there are exceptions. According to Wisner Washam, the writing staff of *All My Children* no longer projects on such a long-range basis; instead, they deal only with the arc of a particular story and do not try to project all the stories of all the characters. In other words, they do a limited projection of approximately twenty-five pages every two or three months. Edith Sommer and Bob Soderberg like to keep a certain amount of flexibility in their projections; they spelled out some of their stories in detail and left others roughed in, i.e., they planned that in two or three months a certain character would be killed, the killer to be decided on at a later date. Ann Marcus confesses that she liked to delay the story conferences and the story decisions as long as possible in order to keep her options open. "I liked to fool myself," she says. Margaret De Priest, however, likes the story decisions to be specific. She usually asks to meet with the owner and producer of *Days.* "I tell them where my thinking is taking me," she says, "and where I think the money is in the next six months to a year." (By "money," she means audience interest.) *Then* she goes home and writes.

Apropos the writing process De Priest gives some useful information. "I decide what's the main story of the next year. Then the second most important. Then the third. Then cross them over." (Which means she interweaves them.) "It's like writing a novel—about 150 pages." Then she does something that is uniquely her own system: She doubles back to time-table the events so she and the show's executives know exactly what the characters' relationships will be at any given time. "I like," she says, "to have a clear, clean story."

Ann Marcus's approach, during her headwriting tenure, was usually more free floating though similar to De Priest's in certain details. After the story conference, she says, "They [the executives] would leave, and I could just sit down and let it flow. I'd take the leading characters and do their story line . . . then the next most important, and so on . . ."

All right. Now that our new headwriter is back at his typewriter at last, let's consider how his long-range projection will differ from the story conference.

The written version, of course, won't depart from the agreed-upon major story decisions. But it will explore, augment, and elaborate on them. As mentioned in Chapter Two, the average projection runs from 70 to 150 pages. It may differ in length, style, and amount of detail from those written by other headwriters. It may concern itself purely with plot as do those of De Priest, because, as she says, "Everyone already knows the character." It may include painstaking psychological analyses of the characters' actions and development, as do Agnes Nixon's projections (quoted by Wakefield in *All Her Children*). Finally it may be written in the jazzy, provocative style the Dobsons like their shows to reflect, not unlike a pop best-seller.

But there are two things the projection must do. It must give the thrust of the various stories, and it must indicate when each one will "peak" (come to a climax, remember?). The projection works like an orchestration, with certain themes building then receding as subthemes come to the fore. In *Eight Years in Another World* Harding Lemay repeats Irna Phillips's early advice. "Using what was already familiar to me," he says, "she explained that writing a soap is like writing three full-length plays simultaneously: when one reaches the end of the final act of the first play, one is well into the second act of another and beginning the first act of a third."

Long, Hot Summer

Even in the matter of laying out the time schedule, however, our headwriter finds he's not a free agent; there are external considerations he must take into account. Summer, for instance.

Summer? What does that have to do with anything?

Summer is the time when high school and college students are on vacation and likely to be home watching television. And they're going to want stories they can identify with. So for shows airing during the summer, the headwriter must tilt his story toward the youthful audience. Events involving the sons and daughters of the show's principals will suddenly move to the foreground, and young love, licit and otherwise, will crowd its more mature counterpart off the screen.

Headwriters' feelings about this kind of slanting vary. Harding Lemay says, "I've seldom gained much satisfaction writing about young people, who have not lived enough to absorb the joys and sorrows which provide resonant dramatic conflict." But youth audience interest is an article of faith with many executives. P&G feels it's urgent to capture this part of the market, not only because young people buy more toothpaste and shampoo than their elders, but also because once hooked on a Daytime show, young people remain hooked for years. As the twig is bent . . .

Consider the manner in which *General Hospital* meets the challenge of summer demographics. Unlike other soaps, *Hospital* does not substitute young characters for older ones during June, July, and August. Instead an action-adventure story line is introduced—a chase or spy story, for instance, which keeps the show at top pitch, while the regular story lines are quietly simmering in the background. The additional excitement seems to keep the young viewers perfectly happy.

Summer brings the headwriter an additional problem. Before the timing of the various storylines is set in concrete, he needs a chart telling him precisely when each of the show's thirty or thirty-five major actors will be taking their vacations. The televison actors' union contract with the net-

How much will his absence hurt General Hospital*? Tony Geary as the inimitable Luke. ABC photo.*

works provides that actors who have been with a show less than ten years earn two-week vacations for each fifty-two weeks of consecutive employment, and those with longer than ten years' employment, three. In practice, however, most actors who've proven their popularity within the shorter period of time have been able to bargain for at least three weeks off, and surely they deserve it. So it's trouble for the headwriter who plans to bring a particular story line to climax in mid-July without first checking what weeks his leading actor will be in Colorado, fishing!

However, there is one way this problem can be solved, though it's not a popular solution. If story requirements are such that the actor *must* be present for a scene or two during his vacation, the essential material can be written ahead of time and pretaped before he leaves town; it can then be edited into the show at a later date. But this shooting usually takes place during an already long day, and the procedure is hard on an overworked crew. The headwriter is far wiser to plan for such absences well in advance so they can be led up to and accounted for in the intervening scripts.

Murder Most Inevitable

By now our headwriter has laid the groundwork for his youth-oriented summer stories, and he has figured out how to work around the cast's vacation schedules. During the story conferences it had been determined how many of the existing stories to keep and how many to discontinue—which of the characters to send over the cliff—and he has the conference notes remind himself (if he needs reminding) what new story lines have been decided on and how they will interact. Now is the time to plan the steps, physical and psychological, leading up to the next several months' major events.

But wait a minute. The events themselves have already been determined. Isn't it too late for the headwriter to start worrying about things like character and motivation? If action flows from character, as it must—haven't we put the cart before the horse?

Maybe. The more experienced headwriter has the privilege of working out story lines *before* the conference, thus making sure they follow the psychological trajectories of the characters—moving, in other words, from character to action. The new headwriter, employed on a shorter leash, has to work in reverse.

It can be done. Stanislavsky's second-in-command and longtime actor, director, and teacher Michael Chekhov used an acting method called the two condition exercise. He provided the actor with a given action; the actor then had to go backward in time and improvise the justification for the action. Our headwriter faces the same problem. Given a decision that X will murder Y in mid-February (so the always popular trial scenes can take place during the May ratings race) the headwriter must backtrack to evolve the steps leading up to the murder, and so arrive at a provocation for the act.

However, it's not always easy. Suppose, ever since the story meeting that determined on the homicide, the headwriter has been questioning the decision. "But X," he's been telling himself, "is not the *type* to commit a violent act."

Maybe not—under ordinary circumstances. It's now the headwriter's job to make sure the circumstances are *not* ordinary. He must plan a steady and relentless buildup of pressure on X which can then be revealed later at the trial. And if he's worried about inconsistency, his fears may be groundless. I suspect none of us know what we might be capable of in a given situation. Beneath our civilized selves the unreasoning child, the unacknowledged savage, lingers still, else where do nightmares come from?

For all the years of his life on the show X may have been sneaky and deceitful, but he has never lifted his hand in rage against anyone; his methods have always been subtler. The headwriter, to bring X to a point of violence, must subject him to an almost unbearable kind of attrition: humiliation, temptation, or frustrated passion, the full extent of which we have probably not suspected—until the big moment at the trial when the truth comes pouring out in a climactic confession scene, made visual perhaps by a pretaped flashback with voice-over which makes the murder seem not only comprehensible but almost inevitable.

The point is that *given the proper motivation,* any character is capable of almost any act—and it's up to the headwriter, faced with a firm executive decision, to find the motivation.

Perhaps the projection's peak is nothing so melodramatic or even anything that's going to happen in a month. Rather the "peak" is suddenly revealed to have happened last year or long ago. Once that story is out, no one is left untouched; every relationship is altered. Inserting a previously unrevealed backstory has a way of deepening and enriching material that everyone had given up as mined out. This device has the additional advantage of surprise, and the expectation of surprise is something that keeps fans coming back—and back. Predictability is every writer's bugbear.

However, in this matter of information withheld, whether it's who murdered Y, or that Q and R, locked in a bitter corporate battle, are unaware they are actually father and illegitimate son—whatever the revelation, it *must be credible.* It may add a new dimension to a character, but it must lie within the realm of possibility for that character; it cannot represent a complete reversal of all we've known about him. Such a revelation also adds to our surprise and gratification if the writer, during the weeks of buildup to the climax, has dropped a few hints, thrown away seemingly casual lines which we can look back on with sudden understanding: "So *that's* what he meant!" After all, any good whodunit writer, however many false clues and red herrings he puts in the way of the reader, also gives the astute reader a fighting chance to guess the truth.

In this regard, but on a somewhat higher level, I cite E.M. Forster again. "The plot-maker expects us to remember, we expect him to leave no loose ends. Every action or word ought to count; it ought to be economical and spare; even when complicated it should be organic and free from dead matter. It may be difficult or easy, *it may and should contain mystery* [italics mine], but it ought not to mislead . . . . And over it, as it unfolds, will hover the memory of the reader . . . (which) will constantly rearrange and reconsider seeing new clues, new chains of cause and effect and the final sense . . . will not be of clues and chains, but of something aesthetically compact, something which might have been shown by the novelist [read headwriter] straightaway, only if he had shown it straightaway it would never have become beautiful."

In the foregoing pages I have, for the purposes of illustration, mentioned story developments that are melodramatic if not outright bloody. I hope the reader understands that I don't advocate a continual diet of violent events. They are, however, examples of the kinds of proposals that executives or the headwriter might put forth to raise sagging ratings or to beat out the competition. Because heightened suspense—the threat of violence, or a terrible miscarriage of justice, or a hint of domestic catastrophe—does seem to keep the viewers tuned in. When we employ such story devices, we are rendering unto Caesar. And let's face it. Soap opera is a commercial medium, and Caesar—the sponsor—does need rendering to.

However, the headwriter should also keep in mind that the real worth of a soap opera lies in its portrayal of human beings with whom the audience can identify. "You lose something when you settle for pace," says Edith Sommer. "You lose character." Whatever else a show may offer, it must contain people we *love*, people whose joys and tribulations we can share. It must also provide us with people we love to hate, people who offer a continuous threat to the welfare or happiness of those we are fond of. And though the need for suspense is always a given, there can be no real suspense if we don't care about the people we're watching. Above all, we need to *care*.

Dragon's Teeth

I will deal later with the quality and content of Daytime; right now let's get back to our headwriter who is just beginning to get the hang of writing it. While he has been bringing his major story lines to a stunning climax, he has also been planting, in his other story lines, dragon's teeth which will develop into full-fledged conflicts in the future. And all this time, remember, he's laboring under excruciating time pressure because the headwriter he's replacing is leaving the show this weekend, and the moment our newcomer gets executive approval for his projection he has to start writing breakdowns. So he probably stays up all night getting his pages in shape, all 70 to 150 of them; bleary-eyed he hands them to his typist the next morning. He gets a few hours' sleep while the pages are typed and, just before the post office closes, he mails them (express mail) to the show's various executives and to the associate writers. And if the projection elicits changes or corrections from the sponsor or producer, these are circulated afterward as follow-up.

But by now our headwriter has already plunged into the next and perhaps most grueling part of his task, the plotting. He must turn his projection, the broad strokes outline, into five breakdowns a week, each breakdown a blueprint for one day's show. And he must ration himself to a carefully calculated portion of his stories so he won't use them up too fast. Yet he must also make sure that each week contains movement, excitement, and suspense. As he plans the events of each week, he must make sure that *each day* something happens that is new, arresting, and provocative. Because always hanging over his head is the possibility that his viewers will tune out today and *not* tune in tomorrow.

How is the actual writing of breakdowns done? Let's go on to examine a few of the techniques that various headwriters use and also look at the restrictions—relating primarily to production problems and expense—that apply even here.

And while we're about it we can find out how most headwriters, no matter how cabin's, cribb'd, confined they are by these logistics, manage to find in this part of the work pleasure that can almost be described as masochistic. Because virtually to a man—or woman—they seem to enjoy plotting, just as they seem to find excitement in the extraordinary demands of the story conference.

Perhaps the truth is that headwriters are born, not made.

4

Headwriting:
Nuts and Bolts

Just as every headwriter
has his own approach to the long-range projection, he also writes the breakdowns in his own way. We'll get to the individual differences shortly; let's
look first at the similarities. Since each of the week's five breakdowns is in
effect the headwriter's specific set of instructions to his associate writer,
what must it contain?

In the chapter immediately following, you'll find a real breakdown
from a real show: one of the Dobsons' written for an episode of *As the World
Turns.* If you glance at it, you'll see that its heading contains first the *episode
number.* By now, for some of the older shows, these numbers are up in the
thousands and going for the ten thousands. After all, the separate episodes
of a show can't be identified by title; they don't *have* titles. So they're identified by number.

Also included are the dates the show will be taped (VTR date) and
aired—the former, with luck, about six or seven weeks after the headwriter
starts his outlining. But if you think that's a comfortable spread, think again.
It's barely enough, considering the convolutions this piece of material will
go through between its inception as an outline and its taping as a finished
script. Shows have been produced with less lead time, but it makes for pep-
tic ulcers for everyone involved.

The breakdown's heading—or perhaps the title sheet (not included
here)—also gives the date the finished script must get back to the headwriter. This is an urgent date, *not to be missed by a single day,* because in this
hectic assembly line world, the headwriter has every hour of every day
budgeted for a specific job and must know precisely what day he will receive

the week's five scripts so he can edit, clean type, and send them on to the producer. The producer in turn expects to receive them by a specific day so he can check them over, have them copied, and get the week's preproduction process started.

Once upon a time when I first began to write for Daytime, I didn't understand the split-second timing of this sequence of events, and early in my Soap career delivered a script to my headwriter the morning after the night it was due. It's only overnight, I told myself. What's twelve hours?

I never did it again. One learns the hard way.

Back to the outline. It also bears, usually scribbled at the top, the name of the associate to whom it is assigned. At random, you think? Do headwriters deal out their outlines like playing cards?

Far from it. Headwriters are quick to learn the idiosyncracies of their associates; they learn which member of their team writes the best love scenes, which one handles comedy best, and which one action/melodrama. Particularly, they learn which associate can be depended upon to write the most meaningful and suspenseful shows; this is the team member who will in all likelihood be regularly assigned the Friday episode with its suspense-producing hook. The Friday show needs to generate enough tension to keep the viewer on tenterhooks through the weekend so he's sure to tune in Monday.

Some associates write faster than others and have bargained out a contract that guarantees them two shows a week. There's a certain advantage to this: a writer builds up a head of steam on one episode which, if he's assigned to the next one, carries over; it gives him a special thrust, an emotional momentum for his characters. Partly for this reason some headwriters of half-hour shows like to write most or all of their own scripts. Harding Lemay, according to his *Eight Years in Another World,* at one point was writing *four* of *Another World*'s five one-hour scripts—in addition to all his other headwriting tasks. He continued to do this even after the show went to ninety minutes, but his description of these months is harrowing.

Yesterday, Today, Tomorrow

What's the time frame of this script in relation to the script of the day before? The headwriter will indicate on each breakdown whether it is "Same Day" or "New Day." If the action takes place on the same day as the preceding script, he'd better specify whether the action is continuous from yesterday's, or whether there's been a hiatus of a few hours, because this will have a bearing on the emotional states of the various characters. If Mrs. S's questionable past was revealed on yesterday's show, and only a few moments have elapsed before today's, then we can expect her to be reacting, perhaps violently, as we come in on her. Or she may be denouncing. Or retaliating. The nature of her first scene today will spring directly from her last scene of yesterday. On the other hand, if several hours—or several days—have passed, she will have had time to recover her equilibrium and perhaps even begun plotting a way to take the offensive.

Another note about time: the heading on each act must indicate in a general way the time of day, or at least how much time has elapsed since the end of the preceding act, in which case it's up to the associate to work out the specifics. Separate scenes *within* the acts don't need to carry this information because we assume they happen concurrently or within minutes of each other. *Lapses of time occur only between the acts.*

On the subject of time: Aristotle advised that a serious work should "keep as far as possible within a single circuit of the sun . . ." I'm sure the custom in soap opera has nothing to do with Aristotle, but there is an unspoken convention that the action of each episode be contained within a twenty-four hour period. Some headwriters, when asked about this, prove to have been observing the stricture without ever thinking about it. But it does seem to have existed since soap opera began.

Conversely, some shows *stretch* time, taking any number of episodes to cover a single day's action. Not all headwriters approve of this. "I watched one show," says Ann Marcus, "and counted: it took them thirteen weekdays to complete a story that took one day." This sort of timing, she feels, gives shows a dreary look, and she has striven to avoid it. On the other hand, *Days of Our Lives'* current writing team tries to cover no more than an hour and a half of action per episode, or at the most, two hours.

(And then there's the legendary story of the character on an earlier Soap who was pregnant with the same baby for eighteen months.)

The relationship between television time and actual time is a matter of the headwriter's choice, and the current tendency is to strive for rapid pace. The one immutable law seems to be the restriction that no single episode cover more than twenty-four hours' action.

From Limbo to Location

Next—place. The heading of each scene of each act will tell its locale. Budget considerations usually determine how many sets are allowed per episode and how many scene changes altogether. On *Days,* for instance, with a three-minute tease and seven acts, De Priest uses from twenty to thirty scene changes a day, which actually break down to a daily allowance of six sets and two telephone limbos. (A limbo is an infinitesimal portion of a set used by a single character with almost no scenery except what can be included in a couple of square feet: a telephone table and chair, for instance, or a portion of a hallway, or a phone booth. Such sets require minimum effort by the production crew and hence don't quite count as separate sets, though they're useful to cut to when trying to break up the action.)

To avoid letting *Days* look static, De Priest keeps her characters moving from one set to another; this also makes maximum use of the sets she's allowed. "Sometimes," she says, "I'll use people in a private place, like a living room or bedroom, then move them to a public place like a restaurant, and then back to the private place again." The trouble is, she admits, motivation can be hard to achieve. But quick short scenes are now the order of the day, and no headwriter wants to buck the trend.

Apart from the man-hours involved in scene changes, another reason for this restriction on the number of sets is a shortage of studio space. Most sound stages where Soaps are shot have almost every square inch occupied with sets and parts of sets. The Dobsons report that *As the World Turns* found itself so pressed for room that the crew sometimes had to knock down one set and construct another between the morning's shooting and the afternoon's. The producer did his best to accommodate, however—even renting space at another studio when the need was urgent.

In a later chapter on associate writing, I'll discuss the physical limitations of the sets themselves—their lack of size and depth, for instance. At this point, however, let's simply say that the headwriter is severely restricted as regards his sets, and must learn to tell his story within those limitations. And any new set he asks for, he'd better plan to use frequently—to amortize it. To build and furnish a set and then knock it down after just one episode is considered a serious extravagance in a show with a tight budget.

Not all shows have tight budgets, though—at least, not *that* tight. In recent years, as advertising revenues and their corresponding production budgets have increased, and with the development of more sophisticated means of editing tape, something new has been added to Daytime: location shooting. Story lines will take characters to the Caribbean, to Greece, Italy, and Spain—giving Daytime a richer and fuller look, and affording viewers a wish-fulfilling glimpse of distant places. Nevertheless, corners are still sometimes cut: when *As the World Turns* sent Kim, Nick, and Steve to Greece a couple of years ago, the actors were accompanied by a camera crew but no sound crew; the material was shot silent and the sound dubbed in later, at home. Interiors were shot at home in the studio also.

Go Easy on the Actors

Now that we understand the requirements and the limitations of time and place in the breakdowns, let's think about the actors needed to tell this week's stories. The breakdown is very specific about which characters will be used in each scene. They're not necessarily listed in the headings or the separate acts; the prose of the breakdown spells out their presence, and the associate writer who is assigned to this script knows he cannot add or subtract anyone. There are good reasons for this, and they're not just artistic reasons.

But if the show's major characters are under contract, doesn't that mean they're available for any act, in an episode?

Far from it. It isn't just the actors' annual vacation schedules the headwriter needs to be aware of. He must also have a chart of each actor's contractual commitments: how many days he *must* be used, and in some cases, how many days he *can* be used. Most actors have a "pay or play" clause in their contracts, stating the number of appearances they're guaranteed each week; and if they're not used that often, they must be paid regardless. Naturally, producers hate to waste an actor's services if they're paid for. In addition the actors with the most clout have a contractual limit to the number of shows per week that can be demanded of them.

Even when no such limit is bargained for, however, the fact is that actors are perishable. It's unwise to use an actor on an hour show more often than three times a week at risk of burning him out. Only rarely, when a given story is peaking, should an essential character be used for a fourth day, and then only briefly. Remember, he not only works about twelve hours a day when he appears, but he must spend any spare time he has memorizing his next script—no easy task. So the headwriter should be wary of overloading him. (Also, those days an actor does appear, it's wise not to use him in more than four acts, for the same reason.) You can have three directors rotating during the week, but actors, unfortunately, are not interchangeable.

We'll deal later with the emergencies that can arise when an actor leaves the show, or breaks a leg, or otherwise falls victim to life's normal mishaps; and we'll also discuss the frantic extra work these crises can require of the headwriter. We'll also speak later about the curious, unacknowledged collaboration that arises between a show's actors and its writers during the life of a show. Right now, however, let's stay with the headwriter and his breakdowns. How does he actually formulate them?

Nuts, Bolts, and Thumbtacks

The mechanics vary as widely as the breakdowns themselves. Some headwriters (Slesar, Lemay, the Dobsons) use a note-card-and-bulletin-board approach. Each important story development of the week is jotted down on a 3x5 note card. Some headwriters even color code their various story lines on these cards. The cards, affixed by thumbtacks to the bulletin board, can be moved about from act to act or day to day, depending on where they seem to work best. This system also allows one to see at a glance when an act or a day is too light and needs to be filled out. When the whole week's events are all in place on the board, a headwriter will, using the cards as his point of reference, either write or tape the rough-draft break-downs, expanding and refining as he goes.

One initiate headwriter heard about this system, bought himself a bulletin board and a pack of note cards, tried to construct a week's break-downs—and gave up and threw the cards away. His writing habits were too ingrained; he could invent only at his typewriter.

Then there is the simple pencil-and-paper approach. Margaret De Priest says, "I pre-outline in pencil, then do one draft on the typewriter." She feels the plotting is the most important part of headwriting, and spends about thirty hours a week on it. Ann Marcus says, "Monday morning I'd start on my breakdowns, and write about two lines for each scene, penciling in each scene very briefly for each day of the whole week." She seldom went into great detail for the dramatic material, presumably because that was more or less self-explanatory. "But the character and humor scenes, I'd spend more time on." (These, clearly, were her favorites.) Ordinarily she'd finish up the preliminary plotting by late Tuesday, then tape record the ex-panded version for the week. The secretary who transcribed the material, she says, smoothed out her "uhh's" and pauses, and "the finished product looked great." (Incidentally, this secretary persuaded Marcus to let her write a sample script, and as a result, became a member of the associate team.)

How much time do other headwriters spend on their breakdowns? Wisner Washam says he spends one full day on each outline, or five days a week. The Dobsons spend four, and Bob Soderberg, on *Another World,* six—a luxury he could afford because another writer was doing his editing. Soderberg's outlines, on whatever show he may be headwriting, are very full—usually twenty-five to thirty pages for each day's action. These out-lines, remember, are double-spaced, with wide margins on either side where sponsor's and producer's changes can be scribbled in after the fact. The Dobsons' breakdowns average from seven to twelve pages per day.

Inevitably there is an inverse relation between the length and detail of a breakdown, and the amount of editing a headwriter can expect to do on the script written from that breakdown. The more complete the outline, the less likely the associate is to stray from it. Agnes Nixon's outlines (again, as quoted by Dan Wakefield) spell out carefully what the thematic *purpose* of a scene is, though she may give her associate a good deal of leeway in its execution. Frank and Doris Hursley, who created *General Hospital* and the canceled *Bright Promise,* would infrequently describe what the impact of a scene should be, and then say, "Feel free!" (Meaning "Write it as you choose." Given this vote of confidence, the associate felt like Shakespeare.

Harding Lemay stated in his book, "It is almost impossible to write a script from anyone else's outlines. The more gifted subwriters often ignored their specific guidelines and created contradictory situations more to their liking, which had to be eliminated to maintain consistency of character and mood."

That's what makes horse races.

The Plotting Process

Having discussed the various mechanical approaches to plotting, let's talk about the day-to-day development of the story lines themselves. Where does one start?

Most writers start with the week's major event, which often takes place at the end of the Friday show. But that's not always the case because headwriters have learned that viewers get wise to this device and may make a practice of saving their viewing for that Friday climax. Margaret De Priest aims for a Friday hook, but she throws in enough surprises and suspense to keep the audience coming back mid-week. The average viewer's custom of watching a show two-and-a-half times a week, she says, is not enough. Ann Marcus says of the plotting process, "When I knew where I was going, I could plot each week toward a cliff-hanger and work toward it, doing a lot of free-associating." But she says she constructed her stories so people *had* to watch every day.

Sommer and Soderberg usually started with the concept of where they wanted to be by week's end, then filled in the intervening steps. But they too learned not to depend on a Friday hook. And the Dobsons know roughly what the Friday show should be and try to reach it, but they are not wedded to it. "It's good to fool an audience and let the hook happen earlier," they say. "If you have too many predetermined patterns the audience learns to predict them. It's better to have the freedom to seize an impulse."

An infrequent but annoying problem is preemption. If some news

Double wedding on Another World, *with Douglass Watson and Victoria Wyndham as Mac Cory and Rachel Davis, and Chris Rich and Laura Malone as Sandy Cory and Blaine Ewing. NBC photo.*

or sports event of world-shattering importance happens on a Friday, the headwriter is likely to find his hook—which he had carefully built to all week long—supplanted by a baseball game, and his great suspenseful moment airing on Monday instead.

However, let's hypothesize a Friday hook, and stay with our headwriter as he works towards it. Let's remember, too, that that hook represents a development only in our *main* story. There are several secondary stories in the works, plus a couple on the back burner—enough altogether to give us one secondary and three major stories for half the days of the week, with an equal number of *other* stories for the intervening days. That makes at least six story lines, in other words, with a couple more we're not really emphasizing yet which will move to the foreground when we need them. That's a sizable number of story lines, and there must be movement—and conflict—in all of them.

Let's talk about conflict for a moment. In one form or another, it needs to be present or potential in almost every scene. Conflict needn't be physical or even overt; sometimes it can exist in the most seemingly casual scene—when the audience knows, for instance, that though characters A and B think they're devoted to each other, they actually have altogether conflicting goals that are bound to emerge as the story develops. (And by the way, the audience loves to achieve an insight into a situation before the characters themselves do.) A character can be in conflict with another individual, with society, or with one of society's structures (a bank, a town mayor on the take, a land developer), or simply with himself—as in the case of a recovering alcoholic for instance. Every one of us in this world has a goal; we are all striving for *some*thing, and it's statistically impossible for us all to achieve it. An infant wants instant attention, instant gratification, total control of his mother, and his first terrible lesson is that those demands cannot always be met. That infant is present in everyone; and not all of us have learned to sublimate his demands. An overcrowded urban society is full of adult children acting out their frustrations and resentments. Haves and have-nots are locked in an unending battle. Men (and women) struggle for dominance, and other men (and women) struggle to escape that dominance. Marriages break apart; children rebel and leave home. People grow and change, and every relationship has a time bomb ticking within it—the time bomb of changing needs and changing expectations. *There is conflict inherent in every human situation,* and it is the headwriter's task to recognize and make use of it. *Without conflict, there is no drama.*

With this well in mind, the headwriter carries his stories forward—or rather, the inherent conflict *propels* his stories forward. His week's break-

Confrontation on One Life to Live, *with Robin Strasser as Dorian, Ava Haddad as her daughter Cassie, and Michael Zaslow as David Reynolds. ABC photo.*

downs consist of events that will complicate, enrich, and deepen each situation, and move it closer to a denouement. In addition to these incidents, the steps that are needed for purposes of story movement, the headwriter must dramatize the emotional and psychological *impact* of each event on the characters. That's what gives soap opera its special value. Hence the need to get maximum mileage out of everything that happens or threatens to happen.

This is one of the areas in which Agnes Nixon excels. Edith Sommer says of Nixon's work: "She gets every last ounce of suspense from a situation. She tells stories *tellingly.*"

There's one other quality our headwriter needs to include in his plotting. Lope de Vega wrote, "*Always trick expectancy.*" He was talking about surprise, which we've mentioned before as a necessary—no, an urgent—ingredient of good soap opera. No viewer needs to watch a show if he can accurately predict what's going to happen. To repeat: *It is the expectation of surprise that keeps the audience coming back.*

The Headwriter Knows Best

Let's assume that by now our headwriter has finished his plotting for the week; the breakdowns are clean typed and, as I've mentioned before, mailed express to the producer and sponsor for their input before being distributed to the associate writers. At that point there may be a hurried executive conference at the other end, netting a phone call to the headwriter. It's curious to note that executives are far more painstaking with the breakdowns than they are with the finished scripts. These phone calls to the headwriter can last for several hours, especially if the headwriter disagrees with some of the suggestions. When agreement is finally reached, the headwriter scribbles any changes into the wide margins of the breakdowns, Xeroxes the corrected pages, and mails them express to the associates—just as the associates' scripts from *last* week's breakdowns arrive and the headwriter must get back to work editing.

The editing process has been touched on in preceding pages, but we can go into it in more detail here, especially since we are beginning to get a more complete picture of the headwriter's relationship to his material. Though some shows retain a writer just to do the editing, most headwriters prefer to have the final say on the finished script—particularly if they are striving for a special quality on the show. Almost any competent craftsman can pick up errors in continuity between one script and the next. However the headwriter, with his pride of authorship and his special feeling for the characters and their emotional build, probably does the most careful job of editing.

The need for rewrites depends in part on how scanty or how extensive the breakdowns are—and how idiosyncratic the headwriter is. Ann Marcus says she did very little rewriting. "Which must mean," she says wryly, "either that I wasn't as painstaking as I should have been, or I had marvelous associate writers—or I wrote foolproof outlines." She'd like, she says, to think the latter. Wisner Washam has an assistant who edits, but Washam does read a final read-through himself. The Dobsons, except during emergencies like vacations, do their own editing, with special emphasis on keeping clichés *out* and humor *in*.

Occasionally a headwriter rewrites an important scene because he anticipates a need to use part of the scene as *flashback* material—in which case the scene must have a taut center that is self-expanatory. A flashback—a portion of a scene that will be saved for reuse in future shows—needs to be short, pithy, and clear, and it must carry the major emotional impact of the situation. An associate writer is not party to the headwriter's future intentions for the scene; the associate knows only that he has four or five pages in which to develop a highly charged emotional situation, and he builds it like a scene in a play, taking his time and reveling in the luxury. He may be deeply hurt when the script comes back to him with the pivotal scene revised and rearranged. "But what was the matter with the way it *was?*" he asks himself.

The answer is: nothing. The headwriter, however, knew that the heart of the scene would be needed as a flashback in another show the week after next, and its essence had to be contained in a few short excerptible lines. In fact, the headwriter in his revision may have labeled the important portion "Begin Flashback Material" at a key point in the scene and "End Flashback Material" a few lines later, so the production crew would know that when the script was taped, this particular part of it should be stored for future use.

As mentioned earlier, the headwriter must also check the associates' scripts to make sure there is an emotional thrust—a trajectory—in the scenes from Monday through Friday. He must smooth out stylistic differences between one associate's script and the next if the differences are extreme. Finally he must make sure they conform to the breakdowns and that no story point has been lost.

And at last, when the rewrites are finished, the five blue-penciled scripts are turned over to typists and as soon as they're clean typed, they're sent to the producer. (P&G shows require nine or ten copies, several to the headquarters in Cincinnati, a batch to the network and the producer, and a couple for the headwriter to save as file copies.)

No Rest for the Weary (Headwriter)

But now, instead of the getting right to work on the next set of breakdowns, perhaps our writer must interrupt his routine and squeeze in one of the many extra tasks required of him. (You don't think the projection, breakdowns, and editing were *all* he had to do, do you?) He may need to write a detailed character sketch, complete with back story, of a new character who's going to be introduced. Or he may need to write an audition scene for that character. Or he must go to the studio to watch a half-dozen or so hopeful young actors perform that audition scene. Perhaps if he lives in the hinterlands, he'll view tapes of the top contenders and phone in his opinion to the producers. (Some headwriters have final say in the casting process; some can merely express a preference.)

Then there are the frantic revisions of already written scripts to explain that cast on the leading actor's leg (he had a waterskiing accident on his vacation); or the revision of the long-range projection because the leading actress is now five months pregnant, and the director has shot her sitting down, behind a table, or in an overcoat as long as he can; she's *got* to be replaced or written out. (And just as her story was peaking, too!)

Still more taxing are those frantic calls from the set, telling him the company's in the middle of shooting episode #9876 and it's running eleven minutes short, or seven minutes long. At that point our headwriter must drop everything, reread the script in question, and consider what areas can be padded or cut. Cutting is fairly easy; expendable material can be found in every script. But lengthening—at the drop of a hat—is another matter. Generally, our headwriter has several choices. He can rummage through previous scripts for flashback material to insert at some likely point in today's script. If there's no good place for such an insertion, he can create a new scene for the pertinent character, perhaps on a limbo set, engaged in deep thought—and then dissolve back to what he's thinking, which is of course the flashback. Or he can quickly write an extension of one or two of today's scenes, phoning in the new material to the producer so it can be shot today. This is not the ideal solution because it's hard for actors who have already learned their lines to learn additional material on a moment's notice. Probably the best way to solve the problem is to immediately write and phone in one or two new scenes for today's script to be shot *tomorrow.* This means using only actors and sets scheduled for tomorrow—although the company's editor will insert the new material into the tape of today's show, after the fact. Is that clear?

Or depending on the length of the shortfall, the writer may want to use a combination of all of the above.

Please, Mr. Postman

But it's still too soon to relax. In addition to all the foregoing, our headwriter must frequently cope with phone calls from New York because the executives feel that a particular storyline isn't working and want it changed. As evidence, they point to the fan mail.

This brings up another of the headwriter's regular tasks: reading the fan mail. Not the fan mail sent to the actors; that's in a class by itself, and writers and producers tend not to concern themselves with it too much. They *are* concerned with letters sent to the production staff, or to the writers of the show; these are always read, tabulated, and considered, along with the ratings, as an indication of how well or poorly a given story line is doing. (Oddly there is not necessarily a correlation between the mail and the ratings.) Since soap opera is a commercial genre, any slight dip in the ratings or any indication of viewer dissatisfaction will bring worried phone calls and general pressure from the sponsors or network people to hype the story. And this, in turn, presents our headwriter with a recurring predicament: Should he bend with every breeze that blows, or take a position on his particular approach to the show and stay with it?

One headwriter says of these week-by-week fluctuations in audience response: "Yes, you need to listen to them, but you've got to trust yourself as a writer." Another says, "I don't think you can run scared. But moderate swings are to be expected." The Dobsons add, "You can't write what you don't believe. You have to be true to your gut feeling." They feel it's a mistake to hype the plot and destroy character. If the audience response seems to make sense to them, they may trim their sails somewhat, but their general advice is: "Don't panic when the ratings go down!"

And last but not by any means least is one more important part of the headwriter's job: monitoring the show—watching it every day and raising Cain with the producer if its quality is not maintained. The producer cares too about what's on the screen and he wants the show to be effective. But the headwriter is the *parent* of the show; he knows what he's been striving for. If the acting or directing or any of the technical components of the show begin to slip, he must state his objections, loud and clear. He's the one, after all, who ties it all together.

You may wonder by now why anyone even *wants* to be a headwriter. And you have a point. In spite of the fact that they find certain compensations in the job (they must or they wouldn't do it), headwriters are almost unanimous about the difficulties inherent in it. Most of them, when asked, speak of the constant time pressure and the weariness. Sommer worried that fatigue might impair her judgment. The Dobsons worry about maintaining freshness—especially after years of writing Daytime. De Priest worries about not being able to keep up a high level of good drama—of research, logic, and dialogue tailored particularly to each actor. There's always the fear, she indicates, that fatigue might affect her ability to maintain the standards she's set for herself. Marcus says, "You can never write 'The End.' You'd create a marvelous, exciting story—but you couldn't stop with its conclusion; you'd have to get something else going. There was never a hiatus."

And yet, and yet . . .

These same writers speak of plotting as "fun." "It's not hard, because it comes out of character." "You can use the cutting edge of your fantasy." "I love that part of it, that area of problem-solving. . . . Inventing a story that has twists and turns and climaxes, then motivating characters to meet story demands. . . ."

See what I mean about headwriters being born, not made?

Before we move on to the work of the associate writer, let's pause and look at an example of a breakdown. It was written by Bridget and Jerome Dobson for an episode of *As the World Turns*. Keep in mind that the headwriter must write five of these each week, in addition to all his other duties, and that he has usually dictated it on to tape, then had it transcribed. Remember, too, that before he could mail it to the associate writer, he sent it to the producer for changes and suggestions, eliciting the kinds of marginal notes included here.

Here goes. Enjoy.

5

By Way of Illustration

For the benefit of those readers who were not watching *As the World Turns* in late summer 1982, here's a quick recap to make the following outline intelligible.

The wealthy and powerful Whit McColl, recently married to Lisa in a secret ceremony, was mistaken for an intruder by policewoman Margo and given a concussion. He's recovered, but he's angry at Margo and wants to break up her engagement to his stepson Tom. Margo's brother Craig is Whit's employee.

Nick Papadopoulos, Kim's husband, suspecting that his ne'er-do-well younger brother Steve and his stepdaughter Betsy are on a romantic rendezvous, has followed them to a cabin in the mountains. In the midst of an angry confrontation with Betsy, he's had a severe heart attack. Steve has arrived in time to see his brother collapse, and has called for medical help.

Karen, whose mother Cynthia recently had a romance with Dr. David Stewart, has been discovered as the person who tried to break up the engagement of David's daughter Annie and her fiancé Jeff, whom Karen is in love with.

After Steve's call, Dr. Bob Hughes is trying to alert Nick's wife Kim about the heart attack. Kim was once Bob's sister-in-law. Now she works for Stan's detective agency.

Dr. John Dixon was once married to Kim.

Maggie is Margo's and Craig's aunt, and an attorney.

In addition to their marginal notes (in italic), I have included the Dobsons' changes on the body of the text itself.

AS THE WORLD TURNS*

#6821   AIR: WEDNESDAY, SEPT. 8 VTR: TUESDAY, AUG. 31

PLEASE NOTE: IT IS THE SAME DAY AS THE PRECEDING SHOW

ACT I, SALON, SAME TIME AS END OF #6820
Margo, Whit, and Craig are there. Margo asks Whit what he wants with her. Whit laughs and says he wants nothing with her. Margo reiterates that there is nothing he can do to keep Tom and Margo apart. She leaves. Whit fumes. He tells Craig he knows that Craig wants a promotion and wants responsibility. Craig says yes, he does. He says by helping Whit hire Maggie he has shown both his loyalty to Whit and his ingenuity. He thinks he's wasted as a chauffeur. Whit says Craig will not be a chauffeur if he can figure a way to get Margo out of Whit's hair, and that means getting Margo out of Tom's life.

move to tag.

CUT TO: CABIN

Nick is trying to speak to Betsy. He says a few words but he loses consciousness. She is afraid he has died. Steve is beside himself. He tells Betsy that Nick is still breathing, but his pulse is racing. He feels helpless. He holds Nick's hand and keeps saying it's going to be okay. Betsy says Nick came and wanted to take her away from Steve. He was going to drag her away if he had to and she wouldn't go. She yelled at him. She told Nick she loved Steve and hated Nick and that Kim was miserable with him. She says she knows Steve wanted to stop her when he came in, but she couldn't be stopped. She *wouldn't* be stopped. She kept hammering at Nick. She feels terrible. She tells Nick she didn't mean it. *Please* hear her; she didn't mean it.

Steve: You can't die. You're my brother. You can't die.

Steve does whatever Bob told him to do in preceding episode.

ACT II, HOSPITAL CORRIDOR AND WAITING ROOM, A LITTLE LATER
Karen comes to the hospital to find David. She sees Jeff, who is just out of surgery. He's giving some instructions to

Lyla. Karen doesn't really want to see Jeff. She gets up her courage and congratulates him on his marriage. She heard the wedding was beautiful. Karen says she's especially happy for them because Annie's pregnant. Jeff says he knows Karen well enough to know what she did—changing Annie's medical records—caused Karen more pain than it did Annie or Jeff. He feels sorry for her. Karen tremulously tells Jeff that she doesn't want his pity. She is very sincere. She hopes Jeff and Annie have lots of wonderful babies. She wants them to be happy. She thinks now he has what he always wanted and she's glad of that.

He is thrilled to see her.

Strong subtext of his feelings

CUT TO: ANOTHER ANGLE OF THE HOSPITAL CORRIDOR

Bob, before leaving for the lake, tries to call Kim. She must be told. She's not at home. Bob is unable to get an answer and he tells Jeff that Nick may have had a heart attack. He's leaving for the lake where Nick is. The Emergency Room should be alerted and Kim should be told. He's tried to call her and he can't reach her. He's got to go now but she *must* be reached. He'll follow the ambulance in his own car.

CUT TO: SPENCER HOTEL REST/LOUNGE

Stan is alone, eating by himself, when Kim enters. He tells her he's very glad to see her. He was feeling alone and craving companionship, especially Kim. She sits down with him and tells him that she's been thinking that she'd like to take two weeks off. She realizes she has no right to ask him. She has not been working for him long eough to ask for it, but she says she thinks she and Nick need it. Stan is a little surprised and covers his own feelings for Kim. He asks what she needs two weeks off for. She says she thinks they ought to go to Greece. Nick seems very happy and at peace in Greece and perhaps together they can find some happiness again. Stan comments that she's really making a very great effort (privately it hurts him a lot) and Kim says she is. He tells her that he wishes her well.

See Kim's desperation. She is trying but unsure that marriage will work out.

ACT III, HOSPITAL CORRIDOR AND WAITING ROOM, A LITTLE LATER

Karen and David are mid-conversation. Karen feels terrible for causing a rift between David and Cynthia. David leads Karen into the waiting room so they can have more privacy. Karen says that she thinks she's to blame and she feels wretched. David says that the way he feels about Cynthia has nothing to do with Karen or what she did or the fact that she changed Annie's medical records. David says that he has been gradually coming to understand his own mind. It hasn't been easy. He's sorry if the fact that it's been slow has caused Karen or her mother more pain, but he knows that he doesn't feel that he should be Cynthia's husband. Karen is privately upset.

CUT TO: CABIN

Steve and Betsy are desperately trying to help Nick. Nick mumbles and Steve asks what he's trying to say. Nick tells Steve that he wants Betsy, then his voice trails off. John enters and quickly checks Nick. Nick keeps asking for Betsy. John tells him to stop it. Betsy is near tears. Steve puts his arms around her to comfort her. He's aware of how affected she is. He realizes that she is shaking, trembling. He holds her tightly. He tells her that Nick is a strong man. John says they've got to get Nick to a hospital. Why the hell did he have to have a heart attack out in the boondocks? What happened? Betsy can only shake her head and start to cry. John is upset. Steve tries to comfort Betsy. John again asks what happened. Steve explains (lying) that Nick and Steve got into a big argument. Steve says he said some things that made Nick very angry. They got into a fight and this happened. John is frustrated because he can't help Nick more than he is under the present conditions. He asks Steve why the hell Nick and Steve didn't stay away from each other. Nick's eyes open. He sees John and tries to speak. John tells him not to try to say anything but to lie very quietly. Nick won't be silenced. He calls loudly for Betsy. Betsy goes to him, tells Nick she's there. She kneels beside him.

ACT IV, MAGGIE'S OFFICE, IMMEDIATELY FOLLOW-ING

Maggie is working at her desk when Margo comes blasting in. She is angry. She says she's heard that Maggie is working for Whit McColl. Maggie says she has no choice. Maggie tells her why she's working for him. She's working because unless she does work as Whit's lawyer, Whit is going to press charges against Margo. Now he's dropping the charges. This makes Margo even more upset and Maggie says she hates to be in that position. She's not the kind of woman who likes to be forced into anything.

Maggie starts sentence "I think Whit is the most . . ."

For transi-tion

CUT TO: SALON

Lisa says ". . . most wonderful man I've ever met." Lisa and Kim are talking about Whit, how happy Lisa is, and how much fun he is—how she probably won't spend all of her time in Oakdale since Whit has a house in Palm Springs, a villa on the Riviera, and an apartment in New York. Kim laughs and thinks it's wonderful. Lisa realizes that Kim is feeling particularly good herself and Kim says she is feeling good because she thinks she has a way to make her life with Nick even better.

Kim ex-plains why she's there—feels des-perate, doesn't know if it'll work

Less opti-mism

CUT TO: CABIN

Betsy, kneeling beside Nick, saying she's so sorry, so terri-bly sorry and Nick, with difficulty, insists that she promise him, she must absolutely promise. Betsy says yes, she'll promise him anything. Nick says promise him that she'll never see Steve again. She must promise that. Steve says no. Nick reaches towards Betsy's face and asks her to promise. She says, I promise never to see Steve again. He touches her face. He smiles, then his hand falls and he dies.

Nick had sudden enormous pain which makes B. promise

Begin with Stan down and out being beeped by Mag-gie—he goes to phone—Maggie has a business question, then in the same conversation he thinks to ask her to din-ner.

ACT V. MAGGIE'S OFFICE, A LITTLE LATER

Maggie is working at her desk when the phone rings. She

answers it personally because the secretary has gone home and has a TWO-WAY CONVERSATION with Stan, who is on phone in cafe bar. Stan tells Maggie that he's at such and such restaurant, he's had a drink and is eating dinner by himself and he needs the companionship of a beautiful woman. He would be glad to eat a second dinner if she would join him. She is thoughtful a moment and says she'd like that.

CUT TO: CABIN
John has really gone into action now on Nick. He thumps Nick's chest (all medical procedures to be researched for accuracy). ~~He gives Nick mouth-to-mouth resuscitation.~~ He works furiously. Steve and Betsy are nearby. Steve, all the time, is saying Nick won't die; he'll not die. Betsy is totally emotionally strung-out. She prays for Nick. We hear sirens. The ambulance arrives. Bob is following in his car. He enters and confirms with John that Nick is dead. He comforts John saying there was nothing John could do. We see the horror on Steve and Betsy's face. Steve can't believe it.

Local police or fire dept. is there. Also oxygen & they use paddles (?— to be researched)

CUT TO : KIM-NICK LIVING ROOM
Kim enters and calls for Nick. There's no answer. She calls for Betsy and suddenly the house seems so very empty.

Don't make K. a complete bitch

ACT VI, MAGGIE'S OFFICE, A LITTLE LATER
Karen is doing some research when Cynthia enters. Cynthia wants to know why Karen called her to come over. Karen is furious and blasts Cynthia for blaming her for the break-up between David and Cynthia. Karen is not going to take on that guilt. Karen tells Cynthia that she is determined not to let her mother get her down. She has a good future ahead of her. She's going to try to go to law school. She thinks it's time to cut the cord.

K. expresses pain that Cyn has lost David

CUT TO: SALON
Craig and Whit are mid-conversation. Craig is upset at Whit's asking Craig to get into his sister's personal life. Whit says Craig is already involved. He has persuaded Whit not to press charges in a civil suit. That has helped Margo. What is Craig so upset about? It will also help

Begin by showing Craig & Whit enter

Craig: how will that help her?

Margo by getting her on another track, that is to get her life turned away from Tom and also it will give Craig a chance to get a major promotion. If Craig doesn't want the opportunity, if he doesn't have the stomach for it, Craig can forget it. In fact, if Craig feels that strongly about it, he doesn't have to come to work tomorrow.

CUT TO: CABIN
Betsy is nearly hysterical with grief. Steve is totally broken. He tells John and Bob that he was with Nick. He caused Nick to have the heart attack. Bob explains that it isn't Steve's fault. It probably would have happened anyway within a matter of hours or days. Steve is upset that they didn't get a chance to become closer, to become brothers again. He wanted that. Betsy says only that she's so terribly sorry.

ACT VII, CAFE BAR, A LITTLE LATER
Maggie enters and finds Stan. She sits down. The scene should be one of joyful man-woman-type chemistry. They are getting to know each other. Stan is now going to eat a

Add: Maggie assumed he was involved w/ someone. Stan: All one-sided

second dinner just to have the pleasure of Maggie's company. He tells her that he's known a lot of lawyers and never one like her. He tells her he thinks they have a lot in common; they deal with criminals. Isn't that a basis for a friendship? Maggie is flirtatious and needful of company. So is Stan, particularly because he sensed Kim moving away from him (but of course this is not verbalized).

CUT TO: KIM-NICK LIVING ROOM
Kim is getting very anxious. She looks at her watch. She calls the Bistro.

CUT TO: CABIN
Steve asks Bob to take Betsy home. He wants to ride with Nick. Bob says he'll be driving his car and can take Betsy with him, but first he wants to make a call. He wants to call Kim. Betsy is upset at that. Bob comforts her, then tries to reach Kim. The line is busy.

CUT TO: KIM-NICK LIVING ROOM
Kim is on the phone being told that no one at the Bistro

has seen Nick today. She hangs up, puzzled.

CUT TO: CABIN
Steve, in this scene, is very strong, very protective. He tells
Betsy she'll be all right. He tells her that if anyone asks, *he*
was with Nick and arguing with Nick, not Betsy. Betsy, who
is numb, nods. She tells Steve the worst thing she can
think of is telling Kim that she caused Nick's death. Steve
says that's exactly the point. Betsy doesn't have to say that.
She can say it was Steve who was arguing with Nick. Can
she do that? Betsy nods and then she says to Steve that it's
over for the two of them. She should have listened to Nick.
They never should have seen each other. Nick was right all
along. It's over. Steve says that Nick was wrong and they
aren't going to forget that just because he's dead. Betsy
pulls away and says no, it's over. She wishes to God she
had listened to Nick. She is intense. Steve is very troubled.

FADE OUT

If you read the marginal notes, you saw that they served several purposes:
they helped track this episode with that of the day before; they enriched the
scenes emotionally; they built Kim's determination to save the marriage
(adding to the tragic irony of Nick's death at this time), and at one point they
altogether altered Kim's mood, building her concern about the marriage.
Incidentally, on rereading the breakdowns, some of these changes may not
have come from the producer but may have been the Dobsons' own revisions. In any event, they were important to the overall impact of the story.

A couple of the marginal notes serve to illustrate something else. At
the end of the first scene of Act IV, the notes have Maggie angrily ending a
speech, "I think Whit is the most—" and we CUT directly to the beginning of
the next scene in which Lisa is saying (as though completing the sentence),
"—most wonderful man I've ever met."

Why did the Dobsons want the break between the scenes handled in
this way? Their marginal note reads *"for transition."* When a soap opera episode carries three or four story lines, the relationships among the stories
are not always immediately apparent, and cuts from one set of characters to
another can sometimes make the show seem jumpy and episodic. In order
to provide the *appearance* of continuity between disparate scenes, a line of
dialogue is used to end one scene which either refers to the characters in

the following scene or provides a thematic link. It's just a trick—but one that gives a look of smoothness and cohesiveness to the episode. The device is usually suggested by the headwriter, but it may also be supplied by the associate.

In a later chapter we will see how the associate writer assigned to this particular episode adapted one of its scenes into teleplay. But first, let's consider the whole matter of associate writing, which headwriter Henry Slesar calls "almost a collaboration." In fact, many headwriters learned their trade as associates. Where does the associate writer come from? How is he selected? How difficult is it to become an associate, and once hired, how does he function? What special qualities, as a writer, should he come equipped with?

Let's find out.

6

And Now, the Associate

At one time the associate writer was the stepchild of the Daytime assembly line. Even his titles revealed the disesteem he was held in: second writer, dialogue writer or dialoguer—worst of all, *sub*-writer. He was part of a literary chain gang, toiling in lockstep with his fellow associates and receiving in return appallingly little money, no credit, and no recognition. Then slowly, thanks in large part to more than a decade of effort by the Writers Guild of America, he began to emerge as a talent in his own right, his contribution to the finished product finally accorded a measure of respect. His pay per show is still not quite on a par with that of his prime-time peers, but unlike many prime-time writers, he may work straight through the year without the seasonal dips in employment that afflict his nighttime opposite numbers. His minimum salary per one-hour show as of June 1984 is $1,374; he must be listed on his show's credit crawl as often as the director but not less frequently than an average of twice a week for each thirteen-week cycle; and—most astonishing innovation of all—he must be granted two weeks' paid vacation for every fifty consecutive weeks of employment. This was bargained out with the network executives in recognition of the speed and ceaselessness with which the associate writer works, and this development is a tacit admission that writers no less than actors can suffer burnout.

Most associate writers have served long and solid apprenticeships in other types of writing before becoming soap writers, though there are a few exceptions, and they have developed mastery of a difficult and exacting craft. Oddly, not every television writer can handle Daytime. First, he needs a sense of the "rhythm" of Daytime, which is totally unlike that of nighttime.

For this reason a few of the recruits to associate writing come from the cast or production staff of a Daytime show where they've learned some of the tricks of the trade.

Also, a Daytime writer must be able to accept and write within the ncessary boundaries of soap opera; for old-time western, or crime show, or sit-com writers this can prove an impossible restriction. One long-time hand from *Wagon Train, The Virginian,* and *Bonanza* tried writing for a Soap, and he peppered his first script with extra characters and sets his headwriter hadn't called for. He felt—no doubt with reason—that he needed them to tell the story properly, and he couldn't comprehend that a Daytime associate doesn't *have* that kind of freedom. Result: he quickly went back to writing for prime time.

There are other reasons some nighttime writers have trouble converting to Daytime. A prime-timer may become more absorbed with the technicalities of plot than character and find it difficult to write to the "sound" of a show's actors, whereas a Saop writer must first and foremost have an ear for every actor on his show. Some long-time Soap writers refer to this as the show's "melody," and we will, in a later chapter, examine it carefully.

Additionally, nighttime writers are used to driving toward—and arriving at—a resolution. The Daytime associate, following the breakdowns, finds himself moving inexorably toward and then *postponing* the resolution, leaving his story lines unresolved and his characters' situations still fraught with problems. This can drive a nighttime writer crazy. He can't understand that getting there is half the fun, and that Daytime's far more leisurely exploration of character development is at least of equal importance with the show's dramatic events.

What It Takes

Although some Daytime associates come from nighttime programming, it takes a certain amount of adjusting. Earlier we asked what qualities an associate needed to work well in the field. What do their bosses have to say about this question?

Opinions on the subject were aired at a soap opera convention given jointly by Writers Guild East and the American Film Institute early in 1983. Several of the headwriter panelists, when asked whether they wanted an associate with "fresh vision," responded with a firm *no*. Associate writing, they agreed, is curiously selfless. "If you have too much style," they said, "you can't do it. You must be *adaptive*."

Many happy returns. Three generations of Stewarts celebrate, with Henderson Forsythe as David Stewart; Mary Lynn Blanks and Robert Lipton as Annie Stewart Ward and Dr. Jeff Ward; Patricia Bruder as Ellen Stewart—and, of course, the Goldman quadruplets as Annie and Jeff's children. CBS photo.

Adaptive. That's an important adjective for an associate writer to remember, because every headwriter has his own characteristics, every show its own style and pace, its own rhythm, its own melody. It's up to the associate to recognize what they are, and to adapt.

There are, however, qualities that a headwriter welcomes. At the same convention, Paul Avila Mayer spoke of one of his associates, Nancy Ford, as "a poet"—having he said, "sensitivity, humor, the ability to write without clichés." Of Claire Labine who had co-created and was headwriting *Ryan's Hope* with him, and who was also writing some of the show's scripts, Mayer said she has "warmth and compassion for the characters, combined with grace and *an ability to evoke emotion.*" Henry Slesar described associate writing as "an art." And ABC's Jacqueline Smith said, "You need a natural passion for it. You must know it's *your form.*"

The consensus, then, seems to be that while an associate needs to merge his own special style with that of the show, he should not simply follow the outline slavishly, but rather bring to it insights of his own.

Other past and present headwriters say that in choosing an associate, they look for "a love of the form;" "the ability to form scenes and write dialogue;" "talent, plus enthusiasm for the show;" "someone who can illuminate the characters;" "someone with an ear for how the characters sound." The Dobsons look for a sense of humor and the ability to be fresh without veering off course—and especially, they say, they look for someone "who can get into our heads."

Beyond all that there's something else, something to be engraved on the associate writer's mind. The panelists at the convention agreed that the best soap writers *do not look down on the medium.* "You cannot condescend," they said.

You can't. Ever. Because condescension implies a contempt for the form and a contempt for the audience; and this inevitably presages sloppy, inferior writing—the kind that is a subtle insult to the viewer. The best associate writers, even when they're turning out seventy or seventy-five pages a week, find they must write at the top of their form constantly. They cannot relax their standards for a single show, a single act, a single scene. Otherwise the material suffers.

Let's take it a step farther. The associate writer, no less than the headwriter, *must believe in what he writes.* If there's any lack of sincerity, commitment, or passion, it will communicate itself directly to the viewer, who will find himself becoming disaffected. He may not know *why* he's disaffected—but he is. If the writer doesn't believe in what he writes, how can anyone else?

Dorothy Parker said the same thing, though about her own writing in books and films, not about Soap writing. In a letter written some years ago to a self-deprecatory colleague and reprinted recently in the *Newsletter* of Writers Guild East, she said, ". . . No writer, whether he writes from love or money, can condescend to what he writes. You can't stoop to what you set down on paper; I don't know why you can't, but you can't. No matter what form it takes, and no matter what the result, and no matter how caustically comic you are about it afterward, what you did was your best. And to do your best is always hard going."

Breaking In

As mentioned before, few would-be associates are hired on the basis of material sent "over the transom" (unsolicited and submitted without the imprimatur of an agent or other person known to the recipient). Jacqueline Smith says that if a sample script arrives at ABC unsolicited, it would be first registered (to protect the network in case of a future plagiarism suit), and then it *might* be read—unless it's a long-range projection, in which case it would be returned *un*read. Procter & Gamble's attitude has traditionally been that unless a script comes through an agent, it is *always* returned unread. They, however, in conjunction with Compton Advertising, are now setting up a writer development program, although this program, too, requires that the applicants already be published or produced, and that the submission come through an agent.

Of the several headwriters who spoke at that convention, only Henry Slesar said that he might read an unsolicited sample script. "For one reason, because I'm curious." In general, however, headwriters are so desperately busy eighteen hours a day that they don't like to bother with inexperienced associates; they don't have time to train them.

Also, if a show is fully staffed and the associates' material is good, the headwriter has no need to look for replacements. Unlike nighttime television, the number of associates working in Soaps at any given time is finite. Discounting cable, which is still in a state of flux, and the nighttime once-a-week neo-soaps like *Dallas* and *Dynasty* and *Falcon Crest,* there are only thirteen true Soaps—give or take a new show or a cancellation as this book goes to print. Multiply thirteen by five (the number of shows aired each week), and you'll see what the problem is: not many jobs in the field.

But once in awhile, an opening does occur. What then?

Although the producer or network representative or sponsor may recommend a candidate, and although any of the above may be the employer of record, the actual selection is made by the headwriter, since he's the one who'll have to work with the newcomer and rewrite the material if it's not up to snuff. Word will go out that a show is hiring; out-of-work associates, who've heard it on the grapevine or from their agents, will hurriedly Xerox a sample of their work—a script they wrote for another Soap, a prime-time script, or even a play (but in any event a piece of *dramatic* writing)—and send it to the headwriter through an agent or a mutual friend.

Why the need for intermediaries? Why can't the material simply be mailed cold to the headwriter? What is all this business about nobody reading anything that comes in over the transom?

Because, as I've said before, there's always the threat of a plagiarism suit in even the most innocent cases of plot overlap. There are, after all, only a few basic plots in the world, and in any medium as hungry for stories as soap opera (sixty-five episodes a week, year after year) duplication of ideas is inevitable. The neophyte writer, however, is convinced he has invented the wheel and is likely to consider every wheel he sees as his own brainchild.

In addition, someone—agent, mutual friend, or producer—needs to vouch for the talent and integrity of the writer. What if the candidate's writing sample actually were plagiarism? Or perhaps the writer simply can't write, thus wasting the headwriter's time? A literary agent screens out the questionable or inadequate work, thereby guaranteeing a certain level of quality or competence in the material. So, we have agents.

For some reason agents seem to be more necessary to job hunting on the West Coast than in the East. Unfortunately, it's sometimes as hard to get an agent to read material as it is to get a headwriter to read it. Only a small proportion of agents will even consider material from an unknown writer, though a slightly larger number will consider material referred by someone known to them. And not all of *those* agents know anything about the Daytime market or have any contacts in it. So it's something of a Catch-22.

Nevertheless I have included in the Appendix a list of film and television agents, with asterisks indicating whether or not they read unsolicited manuscripts. It's advisable, though, if one communicates with any of the agencies on the list, to find out whether or not they handle Daytime writing.

No Shortcuts

If you're interested in becoming a Daytime writer you may, over the last few chapters, have begun to feel considerable frustration. What's the point of a how-to book about Daytime writing when it's so difficult to get into it? Yes, it's difficult—but not impossible. I'm trying, as realistically as I can, to indicate what routes to associate writing are altogether closed to the newcomer, and which ones, however roundabout, might conceivably lead him into the general neighborhood of his destination. Let's see what some of those indirect roads might be.

As mentioned before, a working associate writer might emerge from the secretarial or production staff of the show—having acquired, presumably, some knowledge of the way soap opera works and some of the idiosyncrasies of the show. Perhaps he is an actor on this or another Daytime show who's been itching to try his hand at writing and has persuaded one of the network people to recommend him. Or—once in a blue moon—a viewer writes a letter to the producer, analyzing the show with such brilliance and perceptiveness that he is asked to write a sample script. It has been known to happen.

But these are the rarities. Most associates who are hired already have a track record in Daytime, or they come to Daytime from another writing field. For instance, let's look at the backgrounds of the various associates on *As the World Turns* over several years prior to 1983. What kinds of training did they have, and where did they come from?

All of them had Daytime experience. In addition, most had had training in playwriting; one also had written a musical (produced), and one had been a participant in a short-lived Daytime apprentice program at ABC. One was a former headwriter. Another had a background in acting and then in slick fiction and films. One couple had come from prime-time television and, prior to that, from documentary and newspaper writing. One had been a leading actress on another Soap. And one very talented couple had come (respectively) from fiction and playwriting. The point I'm making is that the *best way to break into Daytime writing is through a measure of success in another writing medium,* or at the very least, to have substantial know-how in soap-opera production.

This brings us back to the qualifications necessary for consideration by the P&G-Compton writer development program. An applicant must already be a *professional* writer, not an amateur. He may have worked in film or television. His material *must* be submitted through an agent, and it should not be specific to any show now on the air. If it's a sample written for one of the P&G soaps, for instance, it will *not* be read. Anyone wanting more information may obtain it by writing to Kathy Talbert, Compton Advertising, 625 Madison Ave., New York NY 10022; she will send a leaflet describing the program and its restrictions.

But let's go back to that Daytime convention for a few last words. The consensus of panelists was that paths to associate writing are often serendipitous: a matter of being in the right place at the right time. It can be a great help to know a producer, for instance, or to be typing scripts for a headwriter when one of the associates quits. At least, it helps in terms of getting that first chance. Once there, however, you have to prove yourself, which usually requires both talent and training.

But let's suppose that the writing sample the applicant submitted has impressed the headwriter, even if his credits haven't. He may now be asked to familiarize himself with the show—to watch it daily for awhile so he gets the sound of the characters. (Some headwriters advise a candidate to track a show for a month before even putting pen to paper.) He'll be sent a batch of recent scripts so he'll know the form the show uses and be able to get a sense of the back story; he may even be given some pages of character description and history. Finally, he'll be given a breakdown for a sample script.

A sample script is just that—a sample. It cannot be aired. Under the terms of the Writers Guild's recent contract, a professional writer not experienced in Daytime must be paid 50 percent of Guild minimum for this script, and a writer who does have a history in Daytime, 75 percent. A fledgling writer has no such protection; he is at the mercy of the producer or headwriter, and thus totally dependent upon company generosity for any payment he may receive. His best protection is to qualify as quickly as possible for membership in the Writers Guild so he can demand at least their sample-script rate.

Let's assume, however, that the headwriter was pleased not only with the applicant's writing sample but also with the sample script written to the breakdown he was sent. What comes next?

The applicant will be hired for a six-week trial period. These six weeks are really the acid test. The newcomer can be fired at any point along the line, but if he survives, he will join the writing team's thirteen-week cycle, and thenceforth his contract usually will be for one script a week to the end of the current cycle, renewable for subsequent thirteen-week periods as long as he continues to give satisfaction—or as long as his current headwriter stays with the show.

Character, Consistency, Credibility

Once the associate has become a regular part of the Daytime writing team, what is expected of him in addition to delivering his script on time every week? Naturally, he will exert himself at all times to write at the very top of his craft. But what particular qualities must his scripts contain, week in and week out?

Frank and Doris Hursley, who were in their day known as "Mr. and Mrs. Television," had some very simple advice for associate writers. "Always keep in mind" they said, *"the three C's"—character, consistency, credibility.*

It sounds gimmicky, but think about it. *Character* is certainly the most important word in the Daytime lexicon. Everything else in Soap stems from character.

If the characters aren't *consistent,* they don't really exist as characters at all, but as cardboard figures the writer moves about at will. They'll behave one way on one occasion and quite a different way on another, leaving the viewer frustrated and unconvinced.

As for *credibility*—do I need to elaborate? *We must believe what we're watching.* If we can't believe in the show and its people, we can't possibly care about them; we're merely observers, watching shadow figures move about on the television screen. If we believe them, we become involved and we become participants. We *feel.*

And I would add another C to the list: *Conflict.* Remember, *without conflict, there is no drama.*

Another quality expected of the associate's material is *accuracy.* If his breakdown calls for a courtroom confrontation, or the booking of a suspect at a police station, or a play-by-play scene in an operating room, the material *must be researched.* Before our associate, writing a trial scene, tackles the marking of evidence, he ought to spend a few hours at the local courthouse watching the procedure. And if one of his characters is being booked for a crime, the associate should go to a local station house, introduce himself, and ask a few questions. (That's how I discovered that the reporters in Santa Monica, waiting around the station house for the daily incident report to be posted, play blackjack. A small point, but a bit of local color I'd never have discovered if I'd merely called the station house for my research data.)

On-the-spot medical observation is a good deal more difficult to come by, for obvious reasons. For his medical scenes, the associate may have to depend on the *Merck Manual* and a call to a doctor friend—or a call to the AMA or to the public relations office of the local hospital. He may have to make several such calls to get a complete and accurate picture.

But he'd better make the effort. If he tries to wing it, if he tries to fake a medical or courtroom or any other scene requiring technical accuracy, there are sure to be two or three hundred retired doctors, lawyers, or policemen watching the show, and every one of them will write to the producer, pointing out the mistakes in excruciating detail.

When an important medical story is scheduled to continue for a number of weeks, some headwriters put a doctor on retainer just to advise them of the pertinent facts. And in an operating-room scene, a medical adviser is often on the set, sometimes doing double duty in a walk-on part as an intern or a scrub nurse. This may give a measure of reassurance to the associate whose first-hand knowledge of meningiomas or extramedullary compressive growths may be somewhat limited. Still, he needs to have done his homework, so the dialogue and business he assigns his actors are at least close to the mark.

In this regard, you will find in the Appendix two lists of sources with phone numbers for accurate information on almost any subject.

Staying on the Team

There are also certain daily tasks the associate needs to perform to make sure he remains on the same wave-length with his colleagues and the show itself. The breakdowns alone don't really inform him sufficiently; they're not written in enough detail. He needs to read the scripts sent him daily from the production office: his own and those of the other team members. The reason for reading the corrected versions of his *own* scripts is to find out what changes his headwriter or his producer has made—and then to figure out the *reason* for the changes so he won't make the same mistake again. And he needs to read the scripts of his peers because each one of them enriches the show to some extent, and he needs to be thoroughly aware of any such additions.

For the same reasons, he needs to monitor the show daily, even though he read the mimeo'd version when it arrived several weeks ago. It's important that he not miss a single nuance that might have been added on the set by an actor or director. Watching the show daily also keeps his ear attuned to the "sounds" of the individual actors.

Most important, however: seeing his own work performed on the television screen every week, week after week, is probably the most effective learning process in the world. In no other form does a writer have such prompt and continuous feedback; it will teach him, if he's conscientious, the difference between dialogue on the typed page and dialogue as his actors deliver it. This is often a painful lesson. The writer is likely to watch the show, tormenting himself with thoughts like: "That line's too long. I should have broken it up . . ." "That scene didn't play well. What was wrong with it?" "Karen's dialogue is too arch. She'll lose sympathy . . ." And again, *"Damn it! That scene is too wordy! Why don't I learn?!!"*

And finally, watching the show daily provides total immersion which keeps the writer feeling a part of the whole. That's essential.

If you have been keeping count, you may have figured out that a Daytime associate works on three time tracks: he's involved in the period of time of the script he's writing currently, he's reading mimeo'd scripts about events that took place perhaps three weeks *before*—and he's monitoring shows that deal with events he wrote about three weeks before *that.* Well figure it out. A script he's writing now won't be mimeo'd for three weeks or aired for another three—a six-week span in all. It's enough to give a writer migraine.

And if you think *that's* difficult, think of the headwriter, who has to edit the scripts, too. This gives him *four* time tracks to keep sorted out—not counting the long-range projection!

Keeping current with all those time sequences, however, is only one mechanical problem. A more significant one is that during his term of employment, the associate gives everything but his life's blood to his job. To meet his deadlines, he must subordinate every other factor of his experience—domestic, social, and emotional. He will, as he writes, put to use everything he has ever learned about writing, about life, about people. He will cannibalize every book or play he ever intended to write, resurrect every pertinent experience he ever had, and takes lines from every private, intimate scene he was ever a part of—reliving the most crucial moments of his life and making ruthless use of them. *Nothing* is too sacred to be reproduced on the pages of his scripts. "Writing," Malcolm Lowry is reported to have said, "means turning the worst moments of your life into fiction." And, we can add, into soap opera.

But, if it works, there are rewards—a sense of pride and a feeling of having created scenes that live and breathe. Lela Swift, a director on *Ryan's Hope,* says that directors look forward to "*the golden moment. . . the moment that sings.*" And if our associate has provided the words for that golden moment, he feels, however fleetingly, that all the pressure and the running and the tension have been worth it.

However we're getting ahead of ourselves. Our associate has only just gotten his job; he still has much to learn. He's barely begun to learn the language of Daytime; there are terms used in the genre that he'll need to acquire. Those readers who have had a certain amount of experience in film or prime-time writing may find much of the information in the following chapter superfluous, but even they will encounter traditions and conventions in Daytime that don't obtain in other areas of television, so we'll include everything.

As we've dealt with the nuts and bolts of headwriting, let's now go to the details of the associate's job. Let's start with the beginning of his six weeks trial run and stand at his elbow as he receives a fat manila envelope in the mail—his first batch of breakdowns.

What next? Where does the associate go from here?

7

Building a Boat in a Bottle

Here's where we are. Our brand-new associate writer, having tracked the show for a month, written a sample script, and been hired for the trial period, has just received his first batch of breakdowns. He's assigned to the Wednesday show. It's time to get to work.

But if the breakdown spells out in unalterable detail where, when, and with whom each scene takes place, what's left to do, except to dramatize what the headwriter has written in prose?

Answer: a lot.

First of all, what is the *thrust* of the Wednesday show and, within that trajectory, the thrust of each scene? The show must have a thrust, or it will lie there like a dead bird. It must be going somewhere. There must be movement. The writer would do well to have clearly in mind *what each scene is really about*—what it achieves in terms of the whole episode's developments. Perhaps, as he reads his breakdown, he should make notes in the margins: regardless of what each character *seems* to be doing, or saying, what is he *really* trying to do?

Unless the associate is gifted with total recall, he must go back to the preceding breakdowns (the Monday or Tuesday episode) to remind himself what his characters were up to the last time we saw them. If John and Mary were quarreling in yesterday's show, they're bound to start their scene today with ill-feeling, tension, or bitterness. We start off straightway with an emotional carry-over from yesterday or the day before, just as the headwriter did in his plotting. This is true whether the Wednesday show is a direct continuation of Tuesday's or takes place on a new day, as indicated at the top of the breakdown.

What is John's stated reason for seeking out Mary, as opposed to his *real* reason, or did they just bump into each other in the hospital hall, to the discomfiture of each? What are the unstated feelings between them, as opposed to the amenities they may come up with? (That's known as *subtext,* and we'll go into it at greater length later.)

From whose point of view are we going to tell the scene? Generally, we tell it from the viewpoint of the person on whom the encounter has the greatest impact. Do we open the scene on Mary as she files charts—and see her reaction as John comes suddenly into the shot? Or do we start with John getting off the elevator with fire in his eye, looking for Mary?

Once they meet, how do they act toward each other? It would be easy to have each character come right out and *say* what's on his mind, or how he's feeling. It would be easy—but not nearly so interesting as having each one struggle to keep a lid on his emotions, to talk at right angles to them. Remember that the *expression* of an emotion relieves the inner tension of a scene, and the audience will, unconsciously, relax. Whereas if the emotion is held back, the tension remains. And the fact is, in life most of us are not that confrontational: we struggle to maintain a show of courtesy and normalcy no matter how we may be feeling.

Also keep in mind that the dullest thing in television is talking heads: people in close-up talking at each other. Bridget and Jerry Dobson have a dictum: "Play it, don't say it." The associate needs to remember it's not a radio show he's writing; television provides an image as well as sound, and sometimes an image is more telling than words. Suppose John, who could really kill Mary at this point, manages to keep his anger in tight control as he writes out a new set of orders for a patient—and then we see, in close-up, that in his intensity he has snapped his pencil in two. We are left wondering what this inner rage will drive him to next.

Perhaps we come into the scene when the two antagonists are already going at each other. The headwriter may or may not have indicated how he wants the scene approached. If not, it's up to the associate to figure out how to get the most mileage out of the scene. And that brings up the question of *tempo.*

Pace, Style, Texture

If we are striving for pace and speed, then it's better to come into the scene *in medias res,* in the middle of the thing. Doing this we leapfrog introductions, greetings, the "good mornings," and the "well, well, look who's heres." We have even skipped the outbreak of hostilities and thrust the audience right into the midst of them, as we come in at a high point and build to a point still higher. This kind of storytelling is more and more the accepted method, as Daytime shows strive for today's staccato, rapid-fire prime-time beat. Watch the pace of *General Hospital,* for example.

However, it's wise to match the pace of the show to what's going on in the story. To hype the pace of the scenes is really an exercise in futility if the story lines are not also rushing toward a climax. It makes more sense, in other words, to match style and content.

And if we choose to be elliptical and leave steps out, *the audience can always fill in what's missing.* For years motion pictures were edited to show the audience, in almost tedious detail, how a character traveled from A to B. Starting in 1949 with *The Champion,* starring Kirk Douglas and written by Carl Foreman, a major change in film-making technique took place—or so it seems in retrospect to this observer. Films began using a kind of shorthand. For the first time, the makers of a film assumed that if a character were shown contemplating an action, the film could jump ahead to his completing it, and the audience would have filled in the intervening steps. Daytime Drama was a bit slow to pick up on this technique, but it's very much in use now, giving most of the Soaps a much swifter pace than in Irna Phillips' day, or than they had even five years ago.

There's another decision the associate must make. What is the *texture* of the John-Mary scene? If the headwriter has not indicated precisely what time of day it is, the associate may decide for himself what kind of atmosphere would serve him best. Is it still early morning, the halls echoing, the other hospital personnel momentarily out of sight, thus making it impossible for John and Mary to avoid confronting each other? Or is it that busy mid-morning hour when aides are picking up breakfast trays and when nurses are hurrying by with medication trays? In the latter case, the quiet intensity of the John-Mary scene would be played in counterpoint to the frenzied background activity.

A digression. While every real speaking part must be specified by the headwriter, the extra parts and bits may be provided by the associate. These are known as N/S and U/5 parts—Non-Speaking and Under Five lines; both designations indicate pay categories well below other acting minimums. The associate should, in the interests of economy, use them sparingly—but if they're important for background color or the movement of the scene, he may introduce them even though the headwriter has not mentioned them.

Often the exact time of day has been indicated in the breakdown, making some of the foregoing academic. However, given the time of day, the associate needs to consider what his characters would normally—or not so normally—be doing now. Has John just completed early morning rounds? Has Mary been on night duty, and now almost at the end of her shift? Time exists for all of us, and most people have a daily routine. It enhances our sense of reality if we feel both John and Mary are pursuing their ordinary activities when their uncomfortable confrontation takes place.

If John has just arrived at the hospital, what was it like outdoors on his way here? Is he wearing a raincoat or an overcoat, or is it a summer day and already hot outside? We can either ignore the weather and the time of year, or we can use it as a factor in our story telling—but the existence of weather, like time of day, can add local color and serve to fill out a total picture, giving us more of a sense that all this is really happening. Nothing ever occurs in a vacuum, and a show is enriched if it is related to the world around it, even in mundane ways. (The show always, by the way, reflects the real seasons, and usually Christmas and New Year's.)

The associate also needs to be familiar with the show's regular sets. This doesn't mean he needs to have actually set foot in them—but he needs to have observed the sets carefully as he sees them on the screen so he doesn't throw in a stairway, fireplace or closet where none has ever existed. When in doubt, he should call the headwriter and *ask* if Roger Coleridge's apartment has a fireplace or if an elevator gives onto the waiting room at Cedars Hospital. I've always felt that blueprints of the most-used sets should be furnished the associate writers on all shows.

Playing It Again

Getting back to our hypothetical John and Mary: however their meeting occurred, they now face each other across the counter of the nurses' station. We sense their tension, but some of the audience may have missed their previous confrontational scene. Remember the statistic that the average fan watches the show only two-and-a-half-times a week? He's more likely than not to have missed the episode that explained what's going on today. How to bring him up to date?

In the days of radio serials the announcer did that job for us. He gave the listeners a recap—a recapitulation of the events leading up to the characters' current predicament. But nowadays the writer of television serials has no such prop to lean on. He alone is responsible for the recap. But this device is fraught with hazards. If it is used at all, it must be used in a normal, believable, and dramatically justifiable manner. Recapping past events is the part of associate writing that most tries the ingenuity of the writer. If it is not handled skillfully and not integrated into the dramatic essence of the scene, it will stick out like a sore thumb and is one of the factors that made old-fashioned soap writing so deplorable. Remember Carol Burnett's wonderful satire on recap in "As the Stomach Turns?"

I can't think of any infallible rules for writing good recap. But there is a rule about bad recap. If so much of one line of dialogue calls attention to itself as recap—out with it! If you can't incorporate the necessary information into the fabric of the scene so its very utterance sounds as impulsive as all the rest of the dialogue, don't recap at all! That, in fact, seems to be the trend in today's Soaps. Let the viewer figure out what's going on—or let him tune in more often.

Sometimes the headwriter gives the associate a break and lets him use a *flashback,* obviating the need for recap. A flashback, as mentioned earlier, is a scene or part of a scene from a previous script which has been saved for precisely that purpose. It is used to tell what the character is remembering at this moment, and why he feels as he does. It puts us inside his head and lets us re-experience with him a pivotal moment in the recent or not so recent past. A flashback should not run too long—a minute or so at the most, maybe a page and a half of script, or it loses its impact. If its effect on the character is meant to be subliminal, at the threshold of consciousness, it will only last a moment and disappear almost as soon as we realize it's there. If the character is either suppressing a memory or is unaware of the moment's importance to him, we use subliminal flashback. By the way, this is another technique developed in film and borrowed by television. Whenever we need to provide instant insight into the character's state of mind, or instant motivation, we turn to flashbacks.

There are a couple of limitations on the use of flashbacks, however. Each taped episode is kept only about a month after its air date; then the tape is erased and used again. (I can't tell you the feeling of despair I had when I first learned this. I felt I had *really* written on the wind.) The only exceptions to this practice occur with scenes that a headwriter thinks he may need in the future and he'll so indicate when he edits the script. ("Save for Future Flashback Material.")

Another problem with flashback is the cost.

But how can it cost? Aren't we just reusing a scene that's already been shot?

Yes, but there are other considerations. If a flashback using a certain actor is inserted in a later show in which the actor is *not* working, he must be paid scale, the union minimum. Hence, when a breakdown calls for a particular flashback, the headwriter has usually made sure the day it's used is a day when that actor is working anyway, so there's no extra payment.

A different sort of payment accrues to the director of flashback material. Regardless of whether he's working the day it's used or not, any portion of the tape he directed will, if it exceeds thirty seconds, trigger a small fee, which increases with the length of the flashback.

As for the writer of excerpted material, there's a formula of payments depending on whether he's still employed on the series, and how long the flashback runs. These writers' payments are so complicated that they seem to be ignored by all parties, but provisions for them exist. In any event, all these payment requirements are enough to discourage indiscriminate use of this device.

The decision to use flashback is the headwriter's province. But often, if he's under more pressure than usual, he won't include in his breakdown the script number of the original episode, but only the general action ("We flash back to the scene when John found Mary rifling through his desk drawers.") If that particular episode occurred some time ago, the associate finds himself thumbing through a small mountain of past breakdowns and scripts, trying to find out exactly when the scene happened and who said what to whom. That's why the associate writer *always* keeps the mimeo'd (shooting) versions of every episode. And that's why not only headwriters but associate writers also need a workroom that can accommodate wall-to-wall scripts.

In any event, having located the scene in question, the associate integrates it into his script, more or less as follows:

"HOLD ON JOHN, AS WE:
LAP DISSOLVE TO: FLASHBACK TO EPISODE #2134,
ACT II. Sc. 3, JOHN'S OFFICE, NIGHT. JOHN HAS JUST
FOUND MARY RIFLING THROUGH THE DRAWERS OF
HIS DESK. THEY ARE MID-SCENE."

The associate will then type in as much of the scene as he wants to reuse, ending with:

"END OF FLASHBACK. LAP DISSOLVE TO: JOHN AND
MARY IN PRESENT ACTION, AS HE LOOKS AT HER
WITH ANGER."

The scene then moves on to complete the confrontation or deliberate avoidance of confrontation. The associate will tag the scene with either John or Mary getting off as incisive a line as possible, to make us eager to know where their hostility will lead them, and we *CUT TO* the next scene.

A brief moment of tranquility for **Edge of Night's** *embattled crime fighter Mike Karr (Forrest Compton) and his wife Nancy (Ann Flood). ABC photo.*

Watch the Time

But if we're going to another set and another couple of characters, why a cut and not a dissolve? The answer, again, is *tempo*. In years past, dissolves ended the separate scenes within the separate acts. But a dissolve has come to imply the passage of time, and it slows up the action, whereas *a cut implies immediacy*. It's far better, then, to imply more or less simultaneous or continuous action within each act; it keeps the story going. If each of the show's seven acts (a one-hour show) has two, three, or four scenes, each scene ends with a CUT TO, and each act ends with a FADE OUT; and, of course, FINAL FADE OUT to end the whole episode.

While we're on the subject of cuts, let's mention *the illusion of elapsed time*. (No, I know you've never heard the phrase, because I only just now invented it to deal with one of Daytime's phenomena.) If we leave John on a particular set at the end of one scene, we do not cut directly to him in a different set at the beginning of the next scene. Since a cut implies immediacy, he can't have had enough time to get from there to here. They do it in movies, but not in Daytime. If, however, the locales of scenes 1 and 2 are supposed to be adjacent or nearly so (for instance the nursing station and the third-floor waiting room a few yards away), we can leave him at the nursing station at the end of scene 1 and, when we cut to the waiting room for scene 2, we can have him come into the waiting room—so long as we allow him at least the indication of enough time to cross the intervening space.

If we want John in scenes 1 and 3, we have a bit more leeway. We can discover him in the waiting room at the opening of scene 3—or we can place scene 3 at a greater distance, in the scrub room down on the next floor for example. Even though scene 2 (when our actor was offstage) only runs a page or two, we can cheat and assume the passage of five or six minutes—long enough for him to have taken the elevator and gone down to the surgical floor where he is starting his scrub.

But we can't, *within the same act,* take him half-an-hour across town because that would violate credibility. Even though a viewer is not consciously aware of the actor's offstage movements, his subconscious is keeping track and demands a measure of plausibility.

While we're discussing time, we should pause here and consider the problem of length, since the length of a script translates itself into playing time. On an hour show, there are about twelve minutes of commercials, plus opening signature, station breaks, and long midshow break, and the credit crawl two or three times a week, leaving about forty-eight minutes of actual drama. The format of *As the World Turns* (excerpted in the next chapter) plays at slightly over a page a minute. Why then do we speak of a seventy-page script? Isn't that too long?

Not necessarily. While some shows require less length (*Days of Our Lives* scripts average sixty-two pages), many headwriters, including the Dobsons and Bob Soderberg, have begun asking for seventy-three to seventy-five pages to ensure a fast-moving show. If the scripts must err in some direction and since it's easier to cut than to pad, too long is better than too short. Some associates even anticipate these cuts by indicating the expendable material in brackets.

There are other variables. Short speeches and quick interchanges play faster than long block speeches. Also every director paces his show differently; some like a swift, staccato tempo, while others like to let the camera linger on the actors' reactions. So it's almost impossible to predict how long a given show will play. Most producers time a script and indicate possible cuts before it's mimeo'd; and a stopwatch is *always* used in rehearsals.

Some associates read their scripts aloud to time them and to see how the dialogue sounds; they don't want to be guilty of writing lines that look better in print than they sound out loud.

In matters of length as well as of format, the newly hired associate should be guided by the back scripts the headwriter has provided him with. For the purpose of this discussion, however, we'll continue to speak of a seventy-page script.

But how, the new writer may ask, does one pace the writing so the script comes out at the right length? One can't arbitrarily allot ten pages to each act and divide up the number of pages per scene on an equal basis; every scene has its own intrinsic length. It's best to let each scene play itself out naturally—only making sure as one reaches the beginning of Act V that one is cruising at about the right length for that point in the script (page 40 or so) and trimming one's sails if need be. One can always go back to cut or pad what's already been written. It's also wise to look ahead at the outline material remaining to see if any of the scenes are very short; this too will affect where one ought to be in mid-script.

With practice one develops a sense of length and after a while begins to come in on target automatically. Sometimes—once in a long while—there is simply not enough material in the breakdown to *make* a full script. If the associate is about halfway through and realizes this, he can call the headwriter and ask for an additional scene or two. But be warned: headwriters look sourly on interruptions to their already frantic workday. It might be better for the associate to try to figure out his own possible solutions to the problem, and to call the headwriter with a suggestion already formulated—an idea for a new scene perhaps, or a particular flashback. His boss may not *use* the suggestion, but it does give him the feeling the associate is thinking creatively and is willing to share the headaches.

Two other matters of timing: the first act used as a tease, and the mid-show break.

On many half-hour shows in the past the first act was called a tease or a teaser. It sometimes preceded the show's title, but it was always used specifically to tantalize the viewer into staying tuned in. As a number of shows went to an hour, this custom was retained by some, abandoned by others, and by still others used only for special effect. (*Days of Our Lives* uses a tease in addition to its seven acts. Generally, now either the tease or the first act is used to grab the audience's attention quickly, and on certain shows, to set up the themes for the day, giving a provocative glimpse at each of the stories today's episode will deal with. In that sense the tease is like the overture to an opera, stating in brief the themes that will be developed in full during the body of the work.

The mid-show break is usually a long commercial break and comes at the end of Act III. For an hour show this break is filled with hazards, coming as it does at about the half-hour mark. What if the uninitiated viewer thinks it's the end of the show and tunes out? What if the regular view is insufficiently hooked and switches to a competing show that comes on the air at about that time? To meet these problems, the associate tries to bring in the end of Act III a few minutes *after* the half-hour because the viewer knows the competing show is already under way. In addition, the headwriter has tried to provide the associate with material that will build the end of Act III to such a fascinating point the viewer is compelled to stay with it.

There's more than one way to skin a cat.

Technological Tools

About instructions for the camera . . The thought of this may be somewhat daunting to the untried associate who has not had film or other television experience. But it needn't be.

Naturally, there are the basic directions like FADE IN, FADE OUT, CUT TO, and DISSOLVE THROUGH TO which have already been mentioned. When one is about to go into flashback, as the earlier example indicates, camera needs to be HOLDING ON the face of the person in whose memory the flashback is taking place. But otherwise the writer can keep in mind that camera movements are determined by the director. In the script the writer need only instruct the camera in the most basic ways: "WE OPEN

ON JOHN AS HE STEPS OFF THE ELEVATOR," or "AS JOHN MOVES AWAY, WE HOLD ON MARY, LOOKING AFTER HIM." Once in awhile, for emphasis, the associate may want to indicate a CLOSE-UP (C.U. for short). Essentially, however, if during the writing the associate is visualizing the scene through the eye of the camera, as he should, he will find himself almost automatically telling the camera where it should be at a pivotal point. Apart from this—let the director do it. When two characters are having a phone conversation, for instance, all we need say is, "INTERCUT AS NEEDED FOR TWO-WAY CONVERSATION."

There are a few devices the writer can make use of if he chooses. An INSERT is a close shot of an object important to the story, which is inserted, ex post facto, at whatever point it's needed, and it's usually something inanimate: a map, or a necklace, or a cassette tape, for example. An ESTABLISHING SHOT tells us where we are: it's usually an exterior and has been shot some other time at the cameraman's convenience, and then edited into a scene at its beginning where needed. The surprising thing is that Daytime does such a good job of *implying* place that an establishing shot is rarely needed. A STOCK SHOT is sometimes used as an establishing shot, but it's material provided by stock-shot libraries; this means our own production team doesn't need to spend time and money filming it themselves. You want to indicate that Dick and Jane are flying to London on a VC-10? Use a stock shot of the plane in the air, then cut inside the plane (a couple of rows of seats, a couple of windows, and the stewardess' voice on the P.A. system over shot—all done very cheaply in the studio) for the Dick-Jane scene. There won't be a member of the audience who won't be convinced that Dick and Jane are really on that plane.

One thing about the physical production of Daytime that takes getting used to is the shallowness of the sets. Sound stage space is at such a premium that most of the sets are a miracle of deception. Only as much of a set as is absolutely necessary on a given day is provided; it may be one end of John's office—and the rest of it is nonexistent. So try to restrict the action accordingly. Don't commit the director or cameraman to a panning shot of John moving from one wall of his office to the other because the other wall may not be there. This is why moving shots are far more rare in Daytime than in prime time. There are exceptions; sometimes a network or sponsor may decide to invest a large amount of money in a particular set to give it a look of elegance—a ballroom scene for instance. Nevertheless, sets are continually being broken down and reassembled elsewhere, so it's wise to limit the mobility of one's character. Let the emotion, not the movement, provide the excitement.

As for scenes of chase and physical violence, perhaps because Daytime actors and directors are so aware of the physical limitations of the set, or because they're not used to doing such scenes often, no one seems to handle that sort of thing very well. It's as though a chase-battle-and capture scene is taking place six inches from the edge of the world and the actors are afraid they'll fall off. This is especially true if the set's supposed to be an exterior, but has in fact been built on a soundstage; those bushes just don't look very convincing.

On the other hand, there are technological advances in Daytime that are quite staggering. Let's take a scene of Dick and Jane driving *to* the airport, with glimpses of the passing city visible through the car windows. No, it's not done with mirrors. It's not even done by rear projection, as in film. It's done by Chroma-Key—an electronic process based on color, which filters out everything the cameraman doesn't want to pick up, and puts in the kind of background (pre-shot) which is color-keyed to show up on the tape. The writer can lay a scene in a moving car, and the production team knows how to shoot it so we could swear it's the car moving and not the background.

Day's headwriter Margaret De Priest, on the other hand, thinks Chroma-Key looks phony. Instead, she brings her character into the car, has him jam the key into the ignition—and just as the engine begins to rev, she CUTS, letting the viewer infer the actual driving.

The new writer may find a few other tools useful. He may want to indicate a P.O.V. shot—a Point of View shot, when the camera acts as the protagonist's eyes, discovering or contemplating something or someone. Or suppose our protagonist has been hurt and is fading in and out of consciousness. The writer may want to indicate in a P.O.V. shot that the doctor's face, as seen by our hero, is coming IN AND OUT OF FOCUS. The camera will oblige.

Incidentally, directions for the reading of a line—the *emotional content of the line*—are capitalized, parenthesized, and included in the speech. To return to Dick and Jane:

INT. PLANE, IN FLIGHT. DICK AND JANE ARE IN THEIR SEATS.

DICK
(BEAT. TROUBLED) You're so quiet. (ANOTHER BEAT) You're not sorry, are you?

Associates vary in their use of stage directions. Some use none at all, taking a page out of Hemingway and writing bare action and dialogue, leaving everything else up to the actor. Others—myself included—seem to need such directions to preserve the mood of the scene and to clarify the subtext (see Chapter 11). Another device used by some associates is to indicate, in caps and parentheses, *the unspoken end of a broken speech*. This isn't always necessary; sometimes it's self-evident. But sometimes the director or the actor needs a clue as to what's remaining unsaid:

                              JANE
That we came? No. I was just—("THINKING ABOUT
JOHN") (SHE BREAKS OFF) When's lunch? I'm starved.

Action, unless it comes within the body of the speech, is capitalized but not parenthesized:

    DICK LOOKS AT HER A LONG MOMENT, THEN LEANS
    OVER TO PRESS THE BUTTON FOR THE STEWARD-
    ESS:
                              DICK
We can't speed up lunch, but I'll get you some more pea-
nuts. (SHE GIVES HIM A WAN SMILE. HE CONTINUES
TO LOOK AT HER, WORRIED. AFTER ANOTHER BEAT:)
Okay. What's the problem?

We won't spell out the whole scene, but only the parts of it that are useful to us. Let's say Jane is reluctant to tell Dick what's on her mind, until he pulls from her that she's worried about John. What if he finds out she's making this trip with Dick?

                              DICK
(IMPATIENT) Hey. John's your *ex*-husband, remember?
That's over with. Done. Forget him!

                              JANE
(UPSET) My God, don't you think I *want* to? I can't!
(THEN) He says if I see you—if I have anything to do with
you—he'll take Jimmy away from me.

The last two speeches are examples of our old friend recap. And Jane's speech brings up another point: under what circumstances are we allowed to invoke the name of the Deity? Answer: rarely, and then only when the person who speaks it is under great duress. On some shows, Jane would be allowed her outbreak; on others, the producer might remove it. Sometimes it might be kept if it only occurs once in that day's script. And Christ's name is never, repeat *never,* used as an expletive.

As for *damn* and *hell,* they too should be used only when the speaker is fairly bursting with emotion. There is an enormous number of viewers who simply do not swear, and for the most part we try to respect their sensibilities.

But let's go on with Dick and Jane:

DICK
(STARING AT HER) But he can't! You've got custody!

JANE
(WITH GREAT RELUCTANCE) He says—he has proof—
(SLIGHT BEAT) that you'd be an unfit parent.

At this point the Stewardess (U/5) probably wheels her drink cart down the aisle INTO SHOT and offers them refills; Dick—stunned by the bombshell Jane has just handed him—can say only that all they want is more peanuts. As those of us who've been watching the show know, John is right: there *is* something in Dick's past that won't bear investigation.

Exquisite Frustration

And so on, with today's three or four major story lines intertwined for the balance of the script—one or another of them often seeming about to come to a climax, but usually sidestepping or postponing it, advancing the story a little but in all cases deepening and enriching the character involvements. A nighttime television writer refers to this as "writing sideways," but that's not quite accurate. Story movement *does* take place; the events, though not yet at a peak, have their effect on the characters. By the end of the show, Dick and Jane have arrived at a situation that is worrisome—arresting—provocative. Perhaps Dick, to assuage Jane's concern about her child, persuades her to call home from the London airport to her baby-sitting mother, and *John* answers the phone. We can CUT BACK to Jane's astonished face for a FAST FADE OUT. We leave our viewers in an exquisite frustration, wondering what's going to happen next—almost guaranteeing that they'll tune in tomorrow.

By now the associate has written his FINAL FADE OUT, but he's not through yet. Another task remains (at least for writers of P&G shows): the summary. It is a one- or two-page précis of what happens in today's script, scene by scene. Summaries are useful for the headwriter and the production company for quick back story references, but for most associates, they seem merely a nuisance. However, even for the associate they can serve a purpose. Forced to review his script and write a one- or two-sentence analysis of each scene, he quickly discovers whether the scene says what it was supposed to. Or did it somehow miss the point altogether? In which case, we hope our associate has left himself enough time for a few quick revisions (sometimes it only takes a line or two) to skew the errant scene back on its track. So even the hated summary can prove a useful tool.

At this point let's pause and take a look at one complete scene from an hour show in order to tie together what we've covered so far. Earlier you read one of the Dobsons' breakdowns for an episode of *As the World Turns*. In the next chapter let's see how this writer, then an associate on the show, turned a scene from that breakdown into teleplay form (and I have an ulterior motive in choosing this particular scene, which we'll get to later in the book). What is reprinted here is not from the final version of the shooting script, but it is the material as it came right from the author's typewriter and was shipped, with the rest of the episode, to the headwriters for editing. As I remember, the edited version of this scene differed slightly from what you're about to read—but this draft will serve its purpose.

8

Fashioned from the Blueprint

Let's start with a glance at the cover sheet which accompanied this episode when it was mailed to the headwriters. This is the *writer's* cover sheet; when the final, edited script reaches the production offices and is copied, the shooting schedule is added to it—but that's the producer's province, not the writer's. All a writer needs to list are the items on the following page. The headwriter, when he receives the script, will check the cover sheet as he reads, making sure that no actor or set has inadvertently been left off.

Give it a look, then we'll move on:

AS THE WORLD TURNS

Episode #6821
VTR: TUES., AUG. 31, 1982
AIR: WED., SEPT. 8, 1982

		CAST
Studio 52:	CBS	MARGO
Agency:	COMPTON ADVERTISING	WHIT
Writers:	JEROME & BRIDGET DOBSON	CRAIG
Assoc. Writer:	JEAN ROUVEROL	NICK
Exec. Prod.:	MARY-ELLIS BUNIM	BETSY
Producers:	RICHARD DUNLAP	STEVE
	HEATHER HILL	KAREN
	PAUL LAMMERS	JEFF
Assoc. Prod.:	BRENDA GREENBERG	LYLA
Sponsor:	PROCTER & GAMBLE	HOSPITAL EXTRAS
		OPTIONAL

Sets:

Act I: SALON.
        CABIN.
Act II: HOSPITAL CORRIDOR AND ADJA-
         CENT WAITING ROOM.
         ANGLE OF HOSPITAL CORRIDOR.
         SPENCER HOTEL RESTAURANT-BAR.
Act III: HOSPITAL CORRIDOR AND ADJA-
          CENT WAITING ROOM.
          CABIN.
Act IV: MAGGIE'S OFFICE.
         SALON.
         CABIN.
Act V: SPENCER RESTAURANT-BAR.
        MAGGIE'S OFFICE.
        CABIN.
        KIM-NICK LIVING ROOM.
Act VI: MAGGIE'S OFFICE.
         SALON.
         CABIN.
Act VII: SPENCER RESTAURANT-BAR.
          KIM-NICK LIVING ROOM.
          CABIN.

BOB
STAN
KIM
RESTAURANT-BAR
   EXTRAS OPTION-
   AL
DAVID
JOHN
MAGGIE
LISA
FIRST PARAMEDIC
   (U/5)
SECOND PARAMED-
   IC (U/5)
FIREMAN (N/S)
TWO AMBULANCE
   ATTENDANTS (N/
   S)
CYNTHIA

TIME: IT IS THE SAME DAY AS THE PRECED-
         ING EPISODE.

Now then: at this point we're going to bypass the first two-and-a-half acts of this episode and go directly to ACT III, Scene 2. I suggest before you read it, however, that you check back to pages 56-62, to the corresponding portion of the Dobsons' breakdown, *to see what the headwriter's intent for this scene was.* Then read the scene from the script, to see how the material was translated to teleplay form, and to see what contribution, if any, the associate made in the process. (You may find that you'd have written the scene entirely differently.)

Here we go:

AS THE WORLD TURNS*   #6821 - III - 24

CUT TO: CABIN. AS BETSY LOOKS ON, FROZEN WITH PANIC,
         AND STEVE HOLDS NICK'S HAND—WANTING TO HELP
         HIM AND NOT KNOWING HOW—NICK STRUGGLES
         AGAINST THE PAIN. AS WE COME IN, HE IS MUMBLING
         SOMETHING INCOHERENT

AGAINST THE PAIN. AS WE COME IN, HE IS MUMBLING
SOMETHING INCOHERENT.

                    STEVE
What's that, Nikos? What are you saying?

                    NICK
(HIS EYES CLOSED. A MUTTER) Betsy?

                    STEVE
Yeah, she's here . . . What do you want?

                    NICK
Want to . . . talk to . . Betsy . . (HIS VOICE TRAILS
OFF)

                    STEVE
Sure . . . Bets . . . come talk to him. Nick, here she is, she
hasn't left . . . (AS BETSY HANGS BACK, FRIGHT-
ENED) It's okay, Bets . . . come talk to him . . . (A BEAT,
AS BETSY TRIES TO SUMMON UP HER COURAGE.
SHE'S SCARED NICK'S DYING, AND CAN'T FACE IT.
AFTER A BEAT, SHE COMES SLOWLY TO HIS SIDE)

                    BETSY
Nick? I'm here. What is it you want to tell me?

                    NICK
(FADING AGAIN) Hurt . . . chest . . . so tight . . .
(HE LAPSES INTO SILENCE AGAIN, EYES CLOSED.
BETSY THROWS STEVE ANOTHER PANICKED LOOK:)

                    BETSY
What do I do?

                    NICK
I don't know. Just . . . don't let him get excited.

                    BETSY
I don't know what to say to him.

                    STEVE
(LOOKING AT NICK'S BLANCHED FACE, CLOSED
EYES) I don't think he hears you anyway.

                    BETSY
Why doesn't someone *come?*

We can dream, can't we? Meg Ryan as Betsy and Frank Runyeon as Steve Andropoulos, in CBS's As the World Turns. *CBS photo.*

STEVE

They will. Don't worry. They will.

BETSY

But we need someone *now* . . . (AS IF IN ANSWER, THERE'S A BANGING ON THE DOOR AND IT BURSTS OPEN AS JOHN COMES IN:)

STEVE

Dr. Dixon . . .

BETSY

Oh, thank God!

JOHN

(SIMULTANEOUSLY, AS HE MOVES FAST TO NICK'S SIDE. A PRETENSE OF CASUALNESS, FOR NICK'S BENEFIT) Well, what've we got here? Nick, I hear you don't feel so good. How're you doing? (BUT HE'S AL-READY TAKING NICK'S PULSE, CHECKING HIS PUPILS. NICK, NOT EVEN AWARE OF JOHN'S PRESENCE, MERELY MUMBLES. JOHN GLANCES UP AT STEVE) Did you call the paramedics?

STEVE

Yeah. 'Bout ten minutes ago.

JOHN

(ANNOYED) What's taking them?

STEVE

They're over at Auburn. That was the closest . . .

JOHN

Well, I wish they'd get here. They've got equipment. I don't have a thing, except nitroglycerine. (TO NICK) Nick, can you hear me? It's John Dixon. (NICK, EYES STILL CLOSED, MAY MUMBLE SOMETHING INCOHERENT) Listen, I've got a little pill here, I'm going to put it under your tongue. Just let it dissolve, okay? It'll help the pain. (HE HAS TAKEN A SMALL CONTAINER FROM HIS POCKET) Open your mouth for me, will you? (NICK DOES, THOUGH WE'RE NOT SURE HE HAS ANY IDEA WHO'S SPEAKING TO HIM) That's the ticket . . . Here.

(PUTS A SMALL PILL UNDER NICK'S TONGUE. NICK
TRIES TO SAY SOMETHING) Hey, keep your mouth shut.
I want that stuff to work.

NICK

(NOT WITH IT) Betsy . . .

JOHN

You can talk to her in a minute. Just let that pill dissolve.

NICK

Betsy . . .

JOHN

Nick, she's here. Just . . . lie still and keep your mouth
closed! (DURING THIS, STEVE HAS SEEN THAT BETSY
IS TREMBLING AND NEAR TEARS. HE MOVES TO HER
SIDE AND PUTS HIS ARM AROUND HER, TIGHT, SUP-
PORTIVELY)

STEVE

(SOTTO) Listen, he's a very strong guy. He'll pull out of it .
. .

BETSY

(DOESN'T BELIEVE IT) Will he? Are you sure? (TO
JOHN) John, is he going to be all right?

JOHN

(RESUMING THE EXAMINATION) Well, I'll feel a lot better
when the paramedics get here. What happened, anyway?
Why the hell did he have to have a heart attack out here in
the boondocks?

BETSY

Well, he . . . he got . . . upset . . . (STOPS, UNABLE TO
GO ON, HER EYES FILLING UP WITH TEARS. STEVE
SQUEEZES HER SHOULDER, INTERCEDES:)

STEVE

(TO JOHN) We . . . we got into an argument. Nick and
me. (BETSY THROWS HIM A LOOK OF SURPRISE) I, uh
. . . said some things that made Nick mad, and . . . well,
everything just sort of . . . heated up, and . . . we got into
a fight and this happened.

JOHN

(DISGUSTED) Oh, for God's sake. Why can't you two guys stay away from each other? You know you don't get along . . .

STEVE

I'm sorry!

JOHN

Yeah, well, "sorry" doesn't make it better . . . Here we've got a very sick man, and I've got no damn equipment! (HE IS PROFANE BECAUSE HE'S FRUSTRATED. NICK'S EYES OPEN, AND HE LOOKS UP AT JOHN. FOCUSES. JOHN'S PRESENCE PUZZLES HIM.)

NICK

Dixon?

JOHN

That's right.

NICK

What . . . you doing here?

JOHN

I came because you're sick. Listen, just be quiet, okay? The paramedics are coming and an ambulance is on its way . . .

NICK

Want . . . talk to Betsy . . .

JOHN

I don't want you to talk to anyone. I want you just to lie quiet till we get some help.

NICK

(GETTING AGITATED; TRYING TO PROP HIMSELF UP AND LOOK AROUND) Betsy . . . Betsy! Where are you . . .

BETSY

(GOING TO HIM, FRIGHTENED) I'm *here*, Nick! Be quiet, please . . . I'm here!

NICK

Don't . . . go 'way. Need . . . talk to you . . . Important. Must . . . listen.

BETSY

Nick, I'm listening. Just . . . don't get excited, okay? I'm here. I won't leave you.

NICK

Hand. Where's your hand.

BETSY

(TAKING HIS) Here. Just . . . hang on, okay? Hold my hand, and . . . lie still. That's right. Just . . . take it easy . . .

NICK

(CONFUSED. SUDDENLY, IN GREEK) *Thie . . .*

BETSY

What?

NICK

(AS STEVE SPRINGS FORWARD TO LISTEN) *Thie . . . pame na fegume. E parliria efuge.*

BETSY

What's he saying?

STEVE

He's mixed up. He thinks he's back home . . . on the boat, with Uncle Demetrios . . .

BETSY

But what'd he say?

STEVE

He said . . . "Uncle, let's go. The tide's going out." (HE AND BETSY LOOK AT EACH OTHER, TOUCHED AND SCARED, AS WE:)

FADE OUT

In the matter of Nick's reverting to Greek as he lies dying: it seemed to me that someone born and brought up in Greece would speak his first language, not his acquired language, on his deathbed. His family were fishermen, so there's logic behind those last few lines. In a later chapter I'll discuss the use of the image, "the tide's going out." In addition, this and subsequent scenes involving the measures taken to try to save Nick's life were written only after countless phone calls to doctors, paramedics, and others. Finally, about the use of the "flawed heavy" John Dixon: this is something we'll want to discuss at considerable length in a later chapter on content.

But before moving on, let me make one comment on format. Certain headwriters, including Douglas Marland, prefer the old-time radio format, which runs margin-to-margin and brings an hour script down to thirty-five or forty pages. Let's take the first few lines of the foregoing scene and see what it would look like margin-to-margin.

CUT TO: *CABIN.* AS BETSY LOOKS ON, FROZEN WITH PANIC, AND STEVE HOLDS NICK'S HAND—WANTING TO HELP HIM AND NOT KNOWING HOW—NICK STRUGGLES AGAINST THE PAIN. AS WE COME IN, HE IS MUMBLING SOMETHING INCOHERENT

STEVE: What's that, Nikos? What are you saying?
NICK: (HIS EYES CLOSED. A MUTTER) Betsy?
STEVE: Yeah, she's here . . . What do you want?

An associate just joining a show should always be guided by the format of the back scripts that have been sent him. He'll find he spends an unconscionable amount of time measuring type-spaces, resetting margins and tabs, and retraining his reflexes for changes in spacing and capitalization. The first script on a new show is always a killer, believe me.

But after that it gets easier.

9

The Half-Hour

Until now, we have concentrated almost entirely on the hour show. But there are still five half-hour shows on the Daytime schedule: *Ryan's Hope, Search for Tomorrow, Edge of Night, Capitol,* and *Loving.* The half-hour, you remember, was the form most of the hour shows evolved from, and it, in turn, evolved from the fifteen-minute show.

Apart from length, however, the half-hour Daytime drama differs in other important ways from its one-hour descendants, and this is a good time to discuss these differences.

Consider, for instance, *Search for Tomorrow,* which first aired in 1951. Popular for several decades, it began to find itself outclassed by timelier and, perhaps, more relevant shows; some of NBC's affiliate stations elected not to use it, and this, in turn, depressed its rating. During the late '70s and early '80s, it began to slide slowly toward the bottom of the Nielsens and oblivion. It was rumored that Procter & Gamble had written it off and was preparing a dramatization of Judith Krantz's novel *Scruples* as a replacement. (A new Soap is rarely commissioned unless there's a time slot available for it.)

What happened at that point is anybody's guess—but at the last moment a decision was made to try to save *Search,* and Procter & Gamble sent in the Marines. The company gave the show a new executive producer, Joanna Lee; a new headwriter, Gary Tomlin; a new team of associate writers—and a new look. Increasingly, the emphasis shifted to fast movement and comedy. The ratings began to edge upward. Whether the remedies were applied in time to reverse the show's several-year trend is a question, but during 1983 everyone connected with the show was optimistic—and determined.

I spoke to a couple of *Search's* recent associates, Robert and Phyllis White, who had been colleagues of mine on a couple of one-hour shows, and asked them what differences they had found, returning to the half-hour form. Was it inhibiting after the relative expansiveness of the longer form?

Maybe. "It makes you more aware," they said, "of the need for concentration. Any character 'widening' has to come as an adjunct of the action that's occurring."

The long-range projections, they told me, are written by headwriter Tomlin, who also does the editing and two of the five weekly breakdowns while an assistant writes the other three. The breakdowns run from seven to ten pages per episode, and according to the Whites, are exceedingly detailed—so much so, creative input by the associate writer is sometimes precluded. The scripts average about thirty-seven pages and include four acts

"Because I tell you to!" Stu Bergman (Larry Haines) tells Jenny Deacon (Linda Gibboney) to take her medicine on Search for Tomorrow. *NBC photo.*

and an epilogue. The full-length first act functions as a tease and each act may average two scenes apiece.

The show carries four basic story lines. Unlike an hour show, which in effect alternates between two full sets of stories, *Search* deals with its major stories as often as four days a week. Additionally, a few characters are "kept alive" for future story developments.

Dancing in a Closet

How about sets, I asked; how many are they allowed? Technically, each episode is budgeted at four sets. But sometimes scenes are shot out of sequence—days or even a week or more after the fact—to take advantage of additional sets being used for other episodes. This kind of advance planning conceals the tightness of the show's budget, and gives a look of much greater production value. There are disadvantages, of course, to this rearrangement of the shooting schedule; there are times when the show's lead time (between script delivery and taping) is actually down to as little as four days, which must be unnerving for all concerned.

Currently, the show is shooting in an old theater on New York's 81st Street, but even the use of this facility shows ingenuity. For a recent warehouse scene, the production struck all the sets and shot against the building's bare interior walls; the sets all had to be reconstructed afterward, but the device worked. The place looked like a warehouse.

Incidentally, viewers of *Search* may have noticed the absence, in the show's new look, of a popular Daytime tradition, the flashback. The reason for this may be that producer Lee comes to Daytime straight from prime time, and she may consider flashbacks a soap-opera wheelhorse she wants to avoid.

This brings up another fast disappearing Daytime convention affecting not just *Search* but many current shows: the voice-over. The VO has customarily been used on a sound track over a close-up of one of the characters to tell the audience what the person is thinking. But as soap opera grows less explicit, and more is left to the audience's intelligence, voice-over may now be going the way of recap; perhaps more and more headwriters consider it too "soapy," and strive not to use it. Anyway, if the actor is good enough, we *know* what he's thinking!

The one-line soliloquy, however, spoken aloud when a character is onstage alone, survives and flourishes. It's rarely used for philosophy or introspection; it's not "to be or not to be," for instance. But it is occasionally used for a punch line. Some headwriters allow it, some don't. An associate writer might try it once or twice, to test the waters, and if it's edited out, he knows that his headwriter objects to it on general principles and that it's a device that shouldn't be used.

Getting back to tight budgets on half-hour shows: there's one headwriter who, at least in the soap-opera phase of her writing career, has written *only* half-hours. Gabrielle Upton has written *Edge of Night, Guiding Light* before it went to an hour, *Search for Tomorrow* at two different periods, and the canceled shows *Love of Life* and *Secret Storm;* she has also served as consultant on others.

In Upton's opinion the *major* problem for the headwriter of a half-hour show is budget. About two-thirds of her writing time, she reports, has been spent planning the most effective use (the amortization) of standing sets, as well as having to bend her story lines to meet actors' commitments or vacation time. Even so, she has found that all these nonwriting digressions often lead to interesting new story twists.

All these considerations, however, apply only during those relatively "normal" periods when a show is shooting in the studio. The planning involved in a location sequence becomes monumental. The interior scenes to be interwoven with the exterior location scenes must all be written and taped before the company ever leaves home; they are edited into the finished product weeks or even months later. And by the way, because until recently she's always worked in the shorter form, she never felt the need for associate writers but always wrote all her scripts herself. Even the *choice* of location may have an economic base: which country, for instance, is most eager to make financial concessions. "You end up," Upton says, "settling for the country willing to pick up the best part of the tab." Imagine the script revisions required when, as happened during her tenure on *Search,* the company changed its location arrangements in quick succession from Majorca to Hong Kong to Jamaica!

In fact, Upton's general comment about being a Daytime writer may strike a chord in those readers with a film or nighttime television background. As one who has always made a living from writing in all media but the stage, she says: "It's as though a ballet dancer were required to perform in a closet with one leg tied behind her."

In spite of this, she admits, the pay is rewarding. And, "Frankly, I have found Soaps can teach a writer to improve his craft."

The Cast of Capitol: 1. Richard Egan 2. Marj Dusay 3. Constance Towers 4. Ed Nelson 5. Deborah Mullowney 6. Christopher Durham 7. Leslie Graves 8. Lana Wood 9. Bill Beyers 10. Julie Adams 11. Nicholas Walker 12. Todd Curtis 13. Tonja Walker 14. Michael Catlin 15. Bradley Lockerman 16. Catherine Hickland 17. Dawn Parrish 18. Rory Calhoun 19. Julie Parrish 20. David Mason Daniels and 21. Kimberly Ross. By permission of John Conboy Productions and CBS.

A Closer Look

Let's take a look at *Capitol,* which was created by Stephen and Eleanor Karpf in 1981. Popular with CBS's affiliate stations, it is carried by almost all of them. For more information about affiliates and why they're important, see Chapter 14.

There are twenty-two minutes of playing time on *Capitol,* the balance of its half-hour going for titles, credits, and commercials. Each episode contains a prologue and three acts, usually with three scenes to an act and the prologue giving a vignette of each of the day's three story lines. The scripts average about thirty-seven pages, and the breakdowns are extraordinarily detailed, averaging about nine pages per episode and providing a good deal of the mood and the color. The script format differs slightly from the P&G format, as you'll see in the pages that follow.

If you've watched *Capitol,* you've seen that it has an expensive patina: sets and costumes look elegant. The show is shot set by set, *not* in sequence; this means fewer setups for the crew, hence quicker and cheaper production. Another important factor in giving the show its look of luxury are those lovely establishing shots of Washington—the Capitol, the Jefferson Memorial, and the Potomac. It's wonderful what magic establishing shots can perform.

I have noticed, by the way, an inverse relation between the amount of budget allotted to a show and the show's need for it. Certainly a show that is struggling with low ratings needs *more* money invested, not less—but here we come up against that seemingly inflexible formula: audience equals ratings equals higher advertising payments equals bigger budget. So *Capitol,* with a comfortable share of the audience in its time slot, looks glamorous and expensive, while *Search,* after more than thirty years of popularity, must make a brave show on a tight budget.

Another interesting fact about *Capitol:* its lead time is rarely more than a week. This, I am told, is deliberate policy on the part of producer John Conboy.

Why? Why would anyone *not* want the security of having several weeks' worth of scripts ahead, ready to be shot?

According to a member of his production staff, Conboy feels that if one of the story lines isn't working, a change of direction can be made quickly and easily without necessitating many rewrites on scripts already completed. The policy makes for greater flexibility and quicker response to audience reaction.

Capitol is headwritten by Peggy O'Shea (*One Life to Live, Search for Tomorrow* and earlier, *Peyton Place*). She is assisted by Craig Carlson;

they do the projections and outlines together. Carlson does some of the teleplays; the associate writing team averages about five writers a week altogether.

O'Shea, incidentally, came to Daytime from writing prime time, like many other headwriters. She pays close attention to fan mail and ratings, and she keeps track of competing shows "to see what's going on there." She chooses associate writers on the basis of sample scripts they've written for another medium, and even then only if they've been recommended by a friend or an agent.

Let's now take a look at the prologue of one of *Capitol's* episodes—first the O'Shea outline from episode #484; then the corresponding scene as dramatized by Craig Carlson. You'll notice that the breakdown is extremely specific, granting the associate very little room for invention.

First a word about the backstory:

Sam Clegg is a powerful Washington industrialist and multibillionaire. Amy Burke, currently afflicted with serious eye trouble, has just discovered he is her father. He has offered to buy off the Burkes in exchange for their staying away from the United States forever.

Zed Diamond is a mystery figure who has arrived in Washington with a lot of money. Ronnie works at his restaurant and is romantically involved with Wally McCandless.

Brenda is Sam Clegg's youngest daughter, trying to forget a brief romance with Wally by dating street-wise young Ricky.

Producer notes are included in the margin.

CAPITOL*

#484
TAPE: FRIDAY 2/3
AIR: TUESDAY 2/14

CAST	SETS
FRAN	AMY'S CLINIC ROOM
AMY	DONATO'S HOTEL ROOM (new)
SAM	ZED'S OFFICE
BRENDA	EXT. MOVIE TICKET LINE
WALLY	LIMBO PHONE BOOTH (ChromaKey)
RONNIE	
ZED	
DANNY	
LOUIE	
BARBER (Zed's) One Shot	
MURDOCK (Voice only)	
EXTRAS AS NEEDED	
3 or 4 Male U/5's	
TAIL (Zed's)	SAME DAY: EARLY EVENING

PROLOGUE/SCENE ONE
AMY'S CLINIC ROOM. A direct continuation from the end of the previous episode as Fran and Amy play out their reaction to the fact Sam Clegg is about to walk in on them. Get a sense of their anxiety about the mutual decision they have made o.c. [off camera] and there's no turning back now. Then Sam enters. His nervousness is increased as he encounters their guarded, hostile stares. Sam assumes this o.c. summons means Amy and Fran have come to a decision. Before they respond, cut to—

PROLOGUE/SCENE TWO
ZED'S OFFICE. A barber is cutting Zed's hair as he converses with Louie. Louie is complaining that she's shown Zed all her best stuff and he keeps giving her the thumbs down. What the hell kind of rock is he looking for when a 15-carat job is too small? Is she out to buy the Hope Diamond, or what? Zed smiles and murmurs that the Hope is a bit much but a lot closer to what he's looking for than the

junk Louie is showing him. They stop conversing at the sound of knock on door. Zed calls for identification and we hear Ronnie's voice announcing herself. Zed whispers for Louie to let herself out the back door and stay in touch. As Louie exits, Zed calls out for Ronnie to enter and as she does, we cut to—

PROLOGUE/SCENE THREE

Brenda does not jump line

Can't see Brenda get out of limo

Bring Ricky into scene

EXT. MOVIE TICKET LINE. Angle from Wally standing somewhere mid-line when his attention is riveted on Brenda exiting from Myrna's limo. Brenda is smashingly dressed (as seen when shopping in the previous episode). She proceeds directly to the ticket booth and attempts to buy a ticket. An irate customer tells her to go to the rear of the line like the "poor people." Brenda realizes her gaffe, mumbles an apology, and sashays down the line, drawing the admiring attention of several guys along the way. Let her run a little gamut of the hey-gorgeous, you-alone? kind of thing and let Brenda respond with cheerful Brenda-style putdowns as she proceeds toward the rear. Play this off Wally's reaction as he hears Ronnie's voice over from Episode #480, stating that Brenda is not sixteen any more—or hasn't Wally noticed? Then as Brenda comes abreast of Wally and he greets her softly, take her surprise and dismay and go to black.

All right. Now let's look at the teleplay version of that prologue:

#484

PROLOGUE—SCENE ONE
FADE IN:
AMY'S CLINIC ROOM
(A DIRECT CONTINUATION FROM OUR LAST SCENE HERE IN #483. ACTUALLY, A MOMENT OR TWO BEFORE, AS FRAN REPEATS HER INSTRUCTIONS TO THE NURSE TO SHOW SAM CLEGG IN)

FRAN
Sister, would you show Mr. Clegg in, please?

(THE NURSE NODS AND EXITS)
(WITH A WORRIED LOOK TO AMY)
Are you all right?

AMY

I've never been so scared in my life.

FRAN

Me neither.

AMY

Do you think we've made the right decision?

FRAN

Honey, I don't know.

AMY

But Mr. Clegg is offering us so much money, and—(I'M
AFRAID, ETC.)

FRAN

(SNAPS, HER NERVES ON EDGE)
Amy, it's too late to—(CHANGE OUR MINDS, ETC.)
(SHE BREAKS OFF AS SAM ENTERS. HE'S CARRYING
A BRIEFCASE. SAM STOPS IN THE DOOR, LOOKS AT
AMY FOR A MOMENT, THEN TURNS NERVOUSLY TO
CONFRONT FRAN'S COLD STARE)
Come in.
(SAM CLOSES THE DOOR BEHIND HIM, REMAINS
STANDING UNCOMFORTABLY)

SAM

You've decided?

FRAN

Yes.

SAM

Fran, I hope you've considered it carefully.

FRAN

Mr. Clegg, please sit down.
(AND AS SAM STUDIES FRAN'S FACE, LOOKING FOR
AN ANSWER . . .)

CUT TO:
PROLOGUE—SCENE TWO
ZED'S OFFICE
(ZED'S DESK HAS BEEN MOVED TO THE SIDE, AND

HE'S PRESENTLY HAVING HIS HAIRCUT. THE BARBER
SEEMS ALMOST INCIDENTAL, HOWEVER, AS ZED
CAREFULLY STUDIES A DIAMOND THROUGH A JEW-
ELER'S LOUPE. LOUIE THE FENCE IS HOVERING
NEARBY, AS)

LOUIE
It's a real shame, Zed. I loved your hair the way it was.

ZED
Quiet, Louie, I'm trying to concentrate.

BARBER
Excuse me, Mr. Diamond. Is this what you wanted—a
more natural (CUT OR)—

ZED
I'm paying you a lot of money, Max. You figure it out.

BARBER
Yes, sir.
(THE BARBER RETURNS TO HIS WORK AS ZED
TURNS THE GEM OVER HIS HANDS, SERIOUSLY STU-
DYING IT)

ZED
Where'd you get this, Louie?

LOUIE
A contact in Memphis. I'm telling you, Zed, the word is out,
all over the country. Guys are calling me, asking who's this
Zed Diamond character? What's he interested in?

ZED
What do you tell them?

LOUIE
Think I'm crazy? I don't tell them nothing. Cause *I'm* the
one who's going to make the score.
(GOING INTO A LITTLE PITCH)
Now, this particular rock is fifteen carats, Zed. It's been in
the market for a few months 'cause nobody can come up
with the big bucks, but I'm sure—(IT'S PERFECT FOR
YOU, ETC.)

ZED

Come in.

(AND AS RONNIE TIMIDLY ENTERS . . .)

CUT TO:

PROLOGUE—SCENE THREE

EXTERIOR MOVIE THEATER

(A SIDEWALK AREA JUST OUTSIDE A MOVIE HOUSE. THERE ARE PEOPLE WAITING IN LINE TO SEE "THE RIGHT STUFF." MIDWAY IN THE LINE IS WALLY, STAND-ING ALONE AND TRYING TO KEEP WARM. IN FRONT OF WALLY ARE TWO YOUNG GUYS, LATE TEENS)

GUY #1

Lucky thing we got here early.

GUY #2

Yeah, the line's going to be around the block pretty soon. (SUDDENLY THEIR ATTENTION, AND WALLY'S, IS DIVERTED BY AN OFF-CAMERA LIMOUSINE PULLING UP IN FRONT OF THE MOVIE)

GUY #1

Check out that stretch limo. Gotta be worth a hundred grand.

GUY #2

Yeah, and check the babe who's getting out of it. (TAKE WALLY'S REACTION AS HE RECOGNIZES BRENDA)

WALLY

Oh no—

(AND ANGLE FROM WALLY AS WE *PICK UP* BRENDA AND RICKY. THEY DON'T SEE HIM)

(BRENDA AND RICKY ARE LAUGHING AND ENJOYING EACH OTHER. WE PICK THEM UP MID-CONVERSA-TION)

BRENDA

You didn't!

RICKY

Yes I did! You think I'd lie about a thing like that? (BRENDA LAUGHS)

114

ZED
(HANDS IT BACK TO A SURPRISED LOUIE)
It's not what I'm looking for.

LOUIE
What the heck are you looking for?! The Hope Diamond?!

ZED
Not quite, Louie. But you're getting closer.

LOUIE
I swear, Zed, you're driving me crazy! I'm showing you the biggest rocks I can find—

ZED
They're not big enough.
(AT THAT MOMENT THERE'S A KNOCK AT THE DOOR)

RONNIE (O.C.)
Mr. Diamond?

ZED
(PROJECTING)
Who's there?

RONNIE (O.C.)
Ronnie Angelo.

ZED
(QUIETLY TO LOUIE)
Take the back door.

LOUIE
What's the big deal? She's seen me here before.

ZED
I've got my reasons, Louie.

LOUIE
Okay, okay. I'll keep in touch.
(TO THE BARBER)
Don't take off too much, Maxie.
(LOUIE COLLECTS HER THINGS AND QUICKLY EXITS.
ZED MAKES SURE SHE'S GONE, THEN)

See! You don't need to spend money to have fun. Stick with me, kid. I'll keep you laughing.

                    BRENDA
(GIVING HIM A HUG)
Thanks, Ricky.

RICKY
(TURNING UP HIS COLLAR OR SOME OTHER GES-
TURE TO KEEP HIM WARM)
Listen, you go stand in line. I'll get the tickets.

                    BRENDA
Wait, this is my treat.

                    RICKY
Get outa here. No way. This movie is required viewing for anybody who hangs out with me. I'll take care of it.
(HE HEADS FOR THE TICKET BOOTH, WHILE SHE SMILES AFTER HIM, THEN STARTS FOR THE END OF THE LINE. AS SHE PASSES A YOUNG GUY, WE HEAR)

                    GUY #3
Hi, gorgeous. I saved a place just for you.

BRENDA
                    No thanks.
(BRENDA MAKES HER WAY TOWARD THE BACK OF THE LINE AS YET ANOTHER SWAIN SPEAKS UP—AND WE INTERCUT WITH WALLY'S REACTION TO THIS)

                    GUY #4
How about stopping right here, beautiful.

                    BRENDA
Sorry, no.
(TAKE A TIGHT SHOT OF WALLY'S REACTION, AND HEAR HIS VOICE-OVER RECALL OF RONNIE, FROM #4XX)

                    RONNIE (V.O.)
Wally, she's not sixteen anymore and she's definitely not a kid, in case you haven't noticed.
(BRENDA GETS TO WHERE WALLY'S STANDING. HE STEPS OUT TO GREET HER)

> WALLY
> Hi, Brenda.
>
> BRENDA
> (SURPRISED, AND SLIGHTLY UNNERVED)
> Oh, hi, Wally.
>
> WALLY
> (OFF HER DISCONCERTED REACTION)
> How are you?
> (AND FROM BRENDA'S MIXED REACTION AT SEEING
> WALLY . . .)
> *FADE TO: BLACK*
> *COMMERCIALS*

And so on to the end of the episode. As you see, the prologue is used in this case to set up the day's three story lines—to provide us with a hook into all three. The pace is taut, the dialogue brisk and natural, and in many of the episodes there is welcome comedy relief. A look at a number of the show's breakdowns reveals that O'Shea establishes in the outlines the pace and tone she wants in the teleplay and she provides a lot of the comedy.

As a matter of fact, the writing schedule on this show is so tight—a day and a half or two days for teleplay—it could not be achieved at all were O'Shea's breakdowns not so complete. Their very explicitness makes it possible and she can take credit for a large proportion of what we see on the screen.

Finally, one more note before we move on, about the show's tight production schedule. Since *Capitol* is produced in Hollywood but its headwriter and story administrators are based in New York, the company uses teletype to transmit its outlines, and its rough-draft and edited scripts, from one coast to the other. This procedure achieves a saving of several days' lead time over the use of even the swiftest express mail system. The shape of things to come.

Now let's take a quick look at some of the other half-hours. Because *Edge of Night* has only recently changed headwriters, I will not go into it here; whenever a new headwriter takes over a show, it takes a while for the dust to settle and the new story lines to manifest themselves. Even the format can be changed.

As for Agnes Nixon's new, early-airing (11:30 A.M. Eastern Time, 10:30 A.M. Pacific) show *Loving,* headwritten by Douglas Marland—that interesting show has broken so much new ground in terms of subject matter that I have chosen to discuss it in a later chapter on content. Unfortunately, *Loving* is in a time slot that has long been regarded by the soap-opera world as Outer Mongolia. Airing at a time when no new Daytime show has ever successfully survived, it seems to be part of ABC's concerted effort to raise its morning ratings. Let's hope it's not a sacrificial lamb.

This brings us to another before-noon show: *Ryan's Hope.* For years there's been a rule of thumb in Daytime that no show airing *before* noon does so well as it might *after* noon: the housewives who made up soap opera's traditional audience in times past were not thought to be through with their household tasks until then. But the audience, as we'll say several times in these pages, is changing, and videotape recorders are making a difference, too.

Let's go on to examine how *Ryan's Hope* has been meeting the changing circumstances.

Complications on Ryan's Hope, *as policewoman Siobhan (Marg Helgenberger) catches sight of ex-husband Joe Novak (Michael Hennessy) while she's on a plainclothes assignment with partner and new lover, Bill Hyde (David Sederholm). ABC photo.*

10

The Half-Hour (Cont'd.)

Created by Claire Labine and Paul Avila Mayer and first aired in 1975, *Ryan's Hope* was the first Soap to deal almost exclusively with a working-class family. Johnny Ryan's bar, in a down-at-the-heels New York neighborhood, reflected an urban reality that many Soap watchers saw nowhere else on television; the Ryan family, says Mayer, "represented the family I would like to have grown up with." Viewers apparently shared the feeling. They watched and identified with the show until 1980 when Labine and Mayer sold it to ABC and later left their posts as headwriters. They returned for most of 1983, but near the close of the year they were replaced once more, this time by Patricia Falken-Smith (*Guiding Light, Days of Our Lives, General Hospital*).

What difference has the change made? Is there a noticeable distinction between the shows written by the previous group and those written by the current headwriter? Under the original headwriters, *Ryan's Hope* took time out occasionally for scenes that had no plot value but explored and expanded character. This, however, may not have been to the general public's taste. According to the show's executive producer, Joseph Hardy, it was felt that the building of suspense and the emotional and confrontational aspects of the show were more important in today's market. "We must keep ourselves moving," he says. "It's better to *act* things out than to *talk* things out."

As for the mechanics, they have not changed substantially. Under Mayer-Labine, the breakdowns were very short, sometimes averaging only three single-space, wide-margined pages per episode (see the pages immediately following). This would seem to be a demonstration of faith in the show's associate writers and their ability to preserve the quality the headwriters wanted. Under Falken-Smith, the breakdowns don't run very much longer, averaging about three and a half pages, but the pages are fuller, more happens, and a great deal more detail is included. Scripts run from thirty-seven to forty pages, but margins are extra wide; there are only about thirty characters to a line. Each episode contains five acts, the first functioning as a tease. The separate acts, which under the former headwriters sometimes consisted of only a single scene, are now often broken up into three or four scenes, making for a faster pace.

At this point it would be interesting to compare excerpts from scripts written for *both* groups; in each case there's a scene from the breakdown and the corresponding scene from the teleplay.

If you're wondering why I'm including so much material from *Ryan's Hope,* it's not only because I think it will be useful to compare differences in style between two headwriting teams, but also because the scriptwriting on this show has been and is still of such a consistently high level, it can only do us good to study it!

First, let's look at the title page:

AMERICAN BROADCASTING COMPANY*
ABC TV-16
433 West 53rd St.
New York, NY 10019
(212) 265-1450

SCRIPT #2165
TAPE DATE: THURSDAY, OCT. 6, 1983
AIR DATE: FRIDAY, OCT 28, 1983

RYAN'S HOPE
Script by Nancy Ford

Story by: Clair Labine
Paul Avila Mayer
Mary Ryan Munisteri
Executive Producer: Joe Hardy
Producer: Felicia Minei Behr
Associate Producer: Nancy Horwich
Directors: Lela Swift
Jerry Evans
Production Assistant: Mindy Steinman

CHARACTERS	SETS	TAPING SCHEDULE (w/#2154 (IB) & #2160 (5A))
Siobhan	I Bill's Apartment/	7:00 - 9:30 Dry Reh.
Bill	Coleridge Living Room	9:30 - 12:00 Block
Maggie	with Front Hall & Stairs	12:00 - 1:00 Lunch
Bess	II Coleridge Living Room	1:00 - 1:15 Notes
Roger	with Front Hall & Stairs	1:15 - 1:30 EPT
Rae	III Bill's Apartment/	1:30 - 5:30 Run & Tape
Frank	Coleridge Living Room	5:30 - 5:45 KD
	IV Roger's Apartment	5:45 - 6:30 Tech.
	V Bill's Apartment	

NIGHT (SAME AS #2164)
(2162-2166)

  The associate writer need not concern himself with the "Taping Schedule" listed in the lower right-hand corner; this is the province of the producer and director. The numbers in the lower left-hand corner (2162-2166) indicate the episode numbers for the week's breakdowns. And this script, as the title page tells us, was written by Nancy Ford (a playwright and former associate writer on *As the World Turns* and *Search for Tomorrow*). The outline was written by Labine, Mayer, and Mary Ryan Munisteri; and its remarkable brevity, as I've said before, can only be a tribute to the headwriters' trust in their associate writers; you'll see that Ford's scene translates it into dialogue that is almost painful in its simplicity and intensity.

  The situation at the beginning of Act V is this:

  Siobhan Ryan Novak had thought she would never see her ex-husband Joe (whom she still loved) again, and had let herself think she was falling in love with Bill, her partner on the police force. Now, however, she has discovered that Joe is back in New York and married to someone else, and she realizes she has never stopped loving him.

  First let's read the headwriters' outline for this, the last act of Episode #2165:

    ACT FIVE - BILL'S APARTMENT - LITTLE LATER.
    SIOBHAN/BILL. While Siobhan finishes packing Bill makes his case. Thinks he is *good* for Siobhan, thinks they are good together; thinks for her to move out on him because of exaggerated feelings of not wanting to be unfair is wrong. Why doesn't she let him decide when he is being unfairly treated? Right now he feels as if Siobhan has a

raging fever and what he wants to do is see her through it to health again. Siobhan appreciates all this but can't remain. Her head is in such a muddle as it is; please don't confuse her. Bill wants to know if this means she will want a new partner? No, is Siobhan's instant answer. No, she doesn't. Bill is relieved at that. Wants her to know he isn't giving up. Siobhan understands that. (Actually doesn't want him to.) Closes her suitcase. Kiss. Goes. Bill looks around; place seems so empty. Notices envelope on floor. One of Joe's letters to Siobhan. He picks it up, is holding it without opening it at tag.

And now, let's read on, to see how Ford turned that paragraph into drama.

rh-2165   5-1

ACT FIVE
BILL'S APARTMENT—SAME TIME
BILL, SIOBHAN
(HE WATCHES, FEELING HELPLESS AS SHE CONTIN-
UES PACKING)

> BILL

Did you eat dinner?

> SIOBHAN

No.

> BILL

I'll fix something.

> SIOBHAN

No.

> BILL

I'll send out for Chinese. We can watch the cop shows while we eat. Count the mistakes. Okay? (SHE TURNS AND LOOKS AT HIM, FIGHTING TEARS, SHAKES HER HEAD) You gotta eat. So do I.

> SIOBHAN

I'm not hungry.

BILL

Okay; you wanta be by yourself to think. Think here. I'll go
to a movie. You need space tonight, you've got it. Right
here. All you want. (HER SILENCE SAYS 'NO.') Then go
up on the roof. Take a blanket and go up on the roof to
think. There's no better place in the city. You're not going
to able to think at your folks' place. Is that where you're going?

SIOBHAN

Probably. (SHE IS ABSENT-MINDEDLY FOLDING A
SHIRT)

BILL

That's mine. (SHE LOOKS CONFUSED) The shirt.

SIOBHAN

I'm sorry.

BILL

No, take it. (SHE SHAKES HER HEAD, PUTS IT ON BED
OR WHEREVER CONVENIENT) *Take* it. (HE PUTS IT IN
HER SUITCASE) If you go, take it. But don't go. (HE
TRIES TO TAKE HER HANDS AWAY FROM PACKING)
Don't go. (SHE HAS TO GENTLY PUSH HIM AWAY)

SIOBHAN

It's not fair to you.

BILL

How do you know? Why don't you let me decide what's fair
to me? (SHE KEEPS PACKING) I say it's not fair to me to
leave. You need me to take care of you.

SIOBHAN

I have to take care of myself.

BILL

You can't right now. You don't know how. To me, it's like
you've got a raging fever and I want to see you through it
till you're well again.

SIOBHAN

I'm contagious; you'll catch the fever. The more you see
me suffer, the more *you'll* suffer. You don't need that.

BILL

Maybe you don't want to get well. Maybe you'd miss the
pain and suffering.

SIOBHAN

That's not fair.

BILL

Let me help you get over him.

SIOBHAN

Thank you. I wish you could—I wish it were that easy . . .
it's not. (SHE CLOSES HER SUITCASE. THEY ARE SI-
LENT, THEN SHE LOOKS AT HIM. REPEATS:) But thank
you. (SHE STARTS TO PICK UP THE SUITCASE)

BILL

I'll do that. (HE TAKES IT OFF THE BED, CARRIES IT TO
THE DOOR AS SHE PUTS A SWEATER OR JACKET ON,
MOVES TO THE DOOR. THEY LOOK AT EACH OTHER)
Does this mean you'll want a new partner?

SIOBHAN

(QUICKLY, WITHOUT THINKING) No. (THEN MORE
THOUGHTFULLY) No, it doesn't. Will you?

BILL

Not on your life. (THEY ARE BOTH CLEARLY RELIEVED)
I'm not giving up though. You understand that?

(SIOBHAN NODS. SHE ACTUALLY DOESN'T WANT
HIM TO. THEY LOOK AT EACH OTHER, AND MOVE IN-
TO A GENTLE KISS. SHE GOES. BILL CLOSES THE
DOOR BEHIND HER, LOOKS AROUND. THE PLACE
SEEMS SO EMPTY. HE NOTICES ENVELOPE ON
FLOOR, GOES TO PICK IT UP, SEES IT IS ONE OF
JOE'S LETTERS TO SIOBHAN. HE HOLDS IT WITH-
OUT OPENING IT)

FADE OUT

Before we go on to another script that aired some four months later,
let's pause to see where the story has taken us in the intervening period.

Joe's wife Jacqueline has learned about the renewal of Joe's affair with Siobhan. Joe has been nearly killed in a bomb blast at Ryan's bar; and Siobhan, pregnant by Joe and fearful of his former underworld connections, knows she must sever her relationship with him. That's why she has agreed to a marriage in name only with her partner Bill—an agreement they've gone to a restaurant to celebrate.

Jacqueline's wealthy and mysterious father, Max DuBujack, has met and is attracted by Siobhan's sister-in-law Jillian, who is married to Frank Ryan.

Jillian, adopted as a child by the wealthy Coleridge family, has recently been reunited with her sister Maggie, who is currently living at the Coleridge house where the self-indulgent Coleridge scion Roger also lives—with the inevitable complications.

Here's the title sheet:

AMERICAN BROADCASTING COMPANY
ABC TV-16
433 West 53rd St.
New York, NY 10019
(212) 265-1450

SCRIPT #2241
TAPE DATE: FRIDAY JANUARY 20, 1984
AIR DATE: MONDAY FEBRUARY 13, 1984

RYAN'S HOPE*
Script by B.K. Perlman

Written by:	Pat Falken Smith
	Mary Ryan Munisteri
	Nancy Ford
	Kathleen Palladino
	B.K. Perlman
	Martha Nochimson
	Peter Brash
Executive Producer:	Joe Hardy
Producer:	Felicia Minei Behr
Directors:	Lela Swift
	Jerry Evans
Production Assistant:	Mindy Steinman

*© Copyright 1984 by American Broadcasting Companies, Inc. Used by persmission.

CHARACTERS	SETS	TAPING SCHEDULE
		(2/#2238 (3D,4A)

CHARACTERS	SETS	TAPING SCHEDULE (2/#2238 (3D,4A))	
Siobhan	I Elegant Restaurant/	7:00 - 9:30	Dry Reh.
Bill	Coleridge Living Room	9:30 - 11:30	Block
Frank	DuBujak Living Room	11:30 - 12:30	Lunch
Jill	II DuBujak Living Room	12:30 - 12:45	Notes
Jacqueline	Elegant Restaurant/	12:45 - 1:00	EPT
Max	Coleridge Living Room	1:00 - 5:00	Run & Tape
Maggie	III Elegant Restaurant	5:00 - 5:15	KD
Roger	Coleridge Living Room	5:15 - 5:30	Tech.
Waiter #1			
(U/5)	IV Coleridge Living Room		
Water #2			
(U/5) 5)	Elegant Restaurant/		
	V Elegant Restaurant		
	Coleridge Living Room		

NIGHT-SAME DAY
(2239-2245)

And now, Pat Falken-Smith's breakdown for Act III of that episode. Note that the act heading lists all the scenes to be used, and all the characters—and there are almost *no* signposts to let us know we're finishing one scene and starting another. The reader must be wary, or he may miss the switch from one scene to the next:

RYAN'S HOPE   2241   Page 2

ACT THREE-ELEGANT RESTAURANT/COLERIDGE LIVING ROOM. SIOBHAN/BILL/FRANK/JILLIAN/WAITER/MAX/JACQUELINE/MAGGIE/ROGER. Bill and Siobhan are enjoying their dinner when Max and Jacqueline enter the restaurant and are seated nearby. Siobhan and Jacqueline see one another, and Bill reacts. He tells Siobhan not to panic. They are not going to let the other Mrs. Novak ruin their celebration. The thing to do is to pretend a lot of excitement and interest in Bill as her date of the evening. He is going to give her the engagement ring right now, because he has it in his pocket. Put it on for the rest of the evening, then she can take it off when they get home. But it certainly will help when word gets out that she's pregnant. The last thing they want is for the DuBujaks to know Siobhan's pregnant. She agrees. He takes the ring out, puts it on her finger and toasts her with wine, quite aware that Jacqueline is observing every moment. Go to Jacqueline as she calls Max's attention to what is happening at the next table. Is it possible that Joe never had an affair with his ex-wife after all? Because it looks very much as if she's getting an engagement ring from Bill Hyde, her partner at the police station. Max glances in their direction, is glad to go along with the theory. They certainly look very much in love. At this moment, bring Jillian and Frank into the restaurant. As they are led to their table by the waiter, they pass Bill and Siobhan and Jillian immediately notices the engagement ring. There is no way out of this for Bill and Siobhan, who ask them to keep the engagement a secret for now, because with all that's happened it doesn't seem like a good time to tell the folks. Frank and Jillian both thrilled for Siobhan and Bill. Go to Jacqueline watching Max watching Jillian. She's the woman he wants, isn't she? Max says yes, she is. He can never hide that sort of thing from Jacqueline. What does she think his chances are? Zero, Jacqueline grins. Mr. Ryan is very attractive, or hasn't Max noticed? Go to Maggie coming home from work, calling out for Frank and/or Jillian and/or Bess. No one answers. She flips the light on in the living room, goes to turn on some music. In a couple of minutes, Roger walks into the room, drink in hand. He's been waiting for Maggie to come home from work. He's still worried about the after-effects from the concussion. He's obviously drunk, and Maggie sees it, but she tries to handle the situation by being very pleasant. Roger wants to examine her eyes, that's the best way to tell about concussions. But, of course, that means he has to come close to her, all right. Of course, he's her doctor isn't he? He smiles. He's been much more to her than her doctor, and he hasn't forgotten a moment of it.

Let's see how the associate writer, B.K. Perlman, translated this into teleplay. By the way, don't be deceived by those initials: the writer is a *she,* and her name is Barbara. Unfortunately there are still employers, more in nighttime episodic than in Daytime, who are convinced that while male writers can write women's stories, women can't possibly write men's stories—so they find excuses for not interviewing them. So a few women circumvent this problem by using only their initials.

RH-2241   3-1

ACT THREE
ELEGANT RESTAURANT/COLERIDGE LIVING ROOM
LATER
SIOBHAN, BILL, FRANK, JILLIAN, WAITERS (U/5), MAX,
JACQUELINE/MAGGIE, ROGER

(UP ON SIOBHAN AND BILL AT TABLE, LAUGHING. HE
OFFERS HER MORSEL FROM HIS FORK. GO TO JAC-
QUELINE AND MAX BEING GREETED BY WAITER)

WAITER

Bon soir, Monsieur DuBujak. Madame. Your table is ready.

MAX

Thank you, Marcel. (AS THEY FOLLOW WAITER) Come,
darling. (AND THEY'RE LED TO TABLE. AS WAITER
SEATS JACQUELINE, SHE SPOTS SIOBHAN. MAX
NOTES HER MOUTH TIGHTEN) What is it? (AND HE
TURNS TO SEE. TAKE SIOBHAN)

SIOBHAN

Oh, God, no—

BILL

(REACHES FOR HER HAND) Take it easy—

SIOBHAN

Of all the restaurants in New York—(PUTS FORK DOWN)
Let's go, Bill.

BILL

Are you kidding? (*RE* HIS FILLED PLATE) You think I'm
gonna ask for a doggy bag in a place like this?

SIOBHAN

I can't pretend she's not there.

BILL

Then pretend the love of your life is *here.* Look at me. Big
broad smile now. (HE SMILES. SHE IMITATES) That's it.
Keep smiling. (TAKES RING BOX FROM POCKET, TALK-
ING THROUGH SMILE) Make goo-goo eyes at me and do
just as I say.

SIOBHAN

(THROUGH PHONY SMILE) My jaw's beginning to hurt. Talk fast.

BILL

Bring your head closer. (SHE DOES, ALMOST NOSE-TO-NOSE) We're gonna get publicly engaged—just for show. I'm gonna put the ring on your finger. Wear it for the rest of the evening.

SIOBHAN

But Bill—

BILL

Take it off when you get home, if you want. (KISSES HER FINGERS) But play lovebirds now for the DuBujaks. They're watching.

SIOBHAN

I bet they are. Like hawks.

BILL

Good. Let 'em think we're the hottest act in town. When they find out you're pregnant, they'll peg me for the father. (SHOWS HER BOX) Here goes. Act surprised now. Lights, camera. Action! (HE OPENS BOX. SIOBHAN PRE-TENDS JOY. TAKE JACQUELINE WATCHING. TAKE BILL PLACING RING ON SIOBHAN'S FINGER, KISSING HER. TAKE JACQUELINE)

JACQUELINE

I can't believe it.

MAX

Stop staring at them.

JACQUELINE

But I thought he was just her police partner.

MAX

Obviously the partnership extends beyond work. (HE LOOKS) Yes, indeed. (TO JACQUELINE:) They're lovers. Longtime lovers, I'd venture.

JACQUELINE

(HOPEFUL) Then maybe Joe never did go back to her.

MAX

From the look on that young man's face—I'd say he'd brook no competition. (GO TO JILL AND FRANK ENTERING, FOLLOWING WAITER TO TABLE, STOPPING AT SIOBHAN AND BILL'S)

JILL

What a nice surprise! (BILL RISES, AD LIBBED GREETINGS BETWEEN THE FOUR. TO BILL:) Please. (SIT DOWN. HE DOES)

FRANK

(TO JILL:) Honey, we're clogging the aisle. (JILL SEES THE RING)

JILL

Wait a minute. Is that . . . (TAKES SIOBHAN'S RING HAND) Frank, look. (HE DOES) Are you two— (SIOBHAN GRINS, NODS)

BILL

I just popped the question.

FRANK

Hey! Congratulations! (SHAKES BILL'S HAND, KISSES SIOBHAN)

JILL

I'm so happy for you. (KISSES SIOBHAN)—BOTH OF YOU.

SIOBHAN

But we're not telling Ma and Da yet.

BILL

We figure one trauma's enough for them this week. (GO TO JACQUELINE WATCHING MAX WATCHING JILL)

JACQUELINE

When a man looks at a woman like that—he'll brook no competition.

MAX

(STARTLED) What?

JACQUELINE

She's the one, isn't she? I know that look in your eyes.

MAX

(SMILES) It's a wise child who pretends not to know her father so well. (A BEAT) Do you think I have a chance?

JACQUELINE

Against her handsome young husband? (SHE SMILES) It's a wise child who keeps her mouth shut. (*GO TO:* MAGGIE, JUST HOME FROM WORK, CALLING:)

MAGGIE

Ma? Anybody home? Frank? (SHE FLIPS LIGHT ON, WALKS OVER TO RADIO, TURNS ON MUSIC, STARTS TO SWAY TO MUSIC AS ROGER WALKS IN, GLASS IN ONE HAND, BOTTLE IN OTHER, DRUNK)

ROGER

I've been waiting for you. (SHE TURNS STARTLED) Beginning to worry about your condition.

MAGGIE

(CAREFUL, AWARE HE'S DRUNK) What condition?

ROGER

(COMING CLOSER) Post-concussion condition. (PUTS BOTTLE AND GLASS DOWN AT DIRECTOR'S CHOICE SPOT)

MAGGIE

Oh, that. I'm fine.

ROGER

I'll tell you if you're fine or not. (HE REACHES HAND TO BRUSH HAIR BACK FROM HER EYES. SHE INSTINCTIVELY SHRINKS BACK)

MAGGIE

What're you trying to do?

ROGER

Examine your eyes. What'd you think?

MAGGIE

Nothing.

ROGER

I'm your doctor, aren't I? I'd hate to think you didn't have confidence in these hands. (SHOWS HER HIS HANDS)

                    MAGGIE
(NERVOUS) I do, Roger.

                    ROGER
Because they're very gentle hands. (TAKES HER FACE IN
HIS HANDS) And they remember every part of you.
(TAKE FRIGHTENED MAGGIE, AND:)
FADE OUT

It's worth noting that *Ryan's Hope* has, during its nine short years of
life, won a disproportionate number of awards from both the Writers Guild
and the Television Academy for best Daytime writing (see Appendix). It's
hard to maintain that kind of excellence, but this show seems to have
done it.

Also worth noting is the wealth of *subtext* in both Ford's earlier script
and Perlman's later one, making this a good time to take up the subject. In
addition you probably noticed the extent to which both associate writers
wrote to the "sound" of the actor who plays Bill. We can now take a look at
the kind of collaboration that early in an associate's employment begins to
grow up between the writer and the actor even though they may never actually meet. What is the actor's contribution to the script, anyway? And how
does learning about the actor's technique help a writer write?

Let's find out.

11

"Speak the Speech, I Pray You . . ."

Sometimes one can succeed in a new job on pure instinct. Or dumb luck, maybe. But there comes a time . . .

Take the author of this book, for instance.

It was the mid-70's. I had been an associate for a year and a half on one Soap and six months on another. I'd also written several screenplays (produced) and a fair amount of slick fiction (published) as well as four books of various descriptions (ditto). In other words, I thought I knew my trade.

But no one had ever mentioned *subtext* to me. Or else the word had gone winging by me, unnoticed.

Then, recommended by a writer friend, I got a job on *Guiding Light.*

I did all the right things. I studied the back scripts the headwriters sent me. I read up on the backstory and sorted out years of relationships, marriages, and divorces. I tracked the show and became thoroughly acquainted with the characters; I began, in fact, to identify with them. And I thought I wrote some first-rate scripts.

But in no time at all they were coming back to me blue-penciled beyond all recognition. Something was wrong.

I studied those edited scripts. Why had my headwriters made so *many* changes? I was following the breakdowns scrupulously, even adding several nice touches. But the scripts that had come back to me had whole pages of the original material x'ed out, and entirely new scenes scribbled into the margins. At this rate I knew the job wouldn't last long—but for the life of me I couldn't figure out what the problem was or how to rectify it.

Worry time.

I mentioned my problem to a neighbor and family friend, actor-coach Jeff Corey. He suggested that if I had trouble with a scene, I could bring it to one of his classes and let his students do an improvisation; it might give me some ideas.

But his classes met weekly, and my deadlines were too tight. Anyway, I could see from the edited scripts that all my scenes were wrong. There wouldn't be time . . .

Then I remembered a remark that my previous headwriter on *Search for Tomorrow,* Ted Apstein, had made recently. "I'm told," I said, "the people from Procter & Gamble have a new favorite word, subtext. Maybe that's what's missing . . ."

"That's how I work," said Jeff. "With subtext."

So, curious but without too much optimism, I started attending his classes as an observer, not a participant. Within a couple of weeks, the edited scripts were coming back with almost no changes at all. And excluding only the period of the Writers Guild strike, I worked for those headwriters for six and a half years. What made the difference?

Subtext.

What did Jeff tell his students, a classful of young actors, that could make such a difference in the way I, a writer, approached a scene?

With his permission (and at risk of usurping some of the material he's using in his own book) I'll include—and we'll analyze—some of the notes I made in those classes. Those, at least, that seem to have as much application to writing as to acting.

Words Left Unwritten

Jeff cites a simple example. Suppose, he says, a friend from acting school has become a director. You need a job. You invite him to lunch, and during lunch you talk about everything in the world except your real goal—that you want a job. That's the one thing you can't say because this lunch is supposed to be strictly social.

The text, then, is what you say. The subtext is what you are *not* saying.

To elaborate: the text is the story. The subtext is the emotional base beneath the words, the accumulation of backstory—and the urgency riding on it. Or, according to Jeff, "ego involvement and ego expectation." What are this character's needs, aims, *expectations* in this scene—and what is the threat to those expectations?

In playing a scene, an actor must look for *the theme, not the story,* he tells his students. Again and again, he reminds them not to play the text of a scene. "If you can't remember your lines," he tells them, "you're not working properly. You're playing the text." The nonverbal content, he says, is what makes a scene interesting. "Acting is richly and largely a nonverbal experience."

How does this apply to writers? Almost literally. A writer should, wherever possible, avoid *writing* the text. "Playwrights," Corey reminds us, "don't write plays just to tell a story—but [even in comedy] to *make a comment about the human condition.*"

And that is what writing Daytime is all about—the human condition.

In playing a scene, he tells his students, an actor must ask himself what a character's *need* is—and it's usually a *primal* need.

Consider an example. A teenager asks his father for money to rent a tux for the sophomore prom. He's nervous because he's afraid his father will get angry at the expense. But what's at stake? Why is it so important?

What's important—and unsaid—is his status with his friends, and what his girl (whom he has already invited to the dance) will think of him if he *doesn't* turn up in a tuxedo. His acceptance by his peer group is at stake. It's almost a rite of passage. And on top of all this, he has fallen in love with that girl. We may call it puppy love, but it's an excruciatingly painful first love. So his primal needs, in this simple request to his father, are profound: a need for tribal acceptance and a desperate need to impress that girl. It's possible that nothing else in his life will ever seem so important.

You see how the scene is instantly enriched? It's still a comedy scene, but underlying it is a young boy's fear of alienation from the group and a fear of loss of love. But perhaps all he says to his father is what the adolescent Mickey Rooney said to Lewis Stone in an early Hardy Family film: "Man to man, Pop, I need twenty bucks."

An actor, then, in preparing a scene should think of relationship and purpose—the theme not the story.

A moment ago I mentioned *urgency.* Jeff tells his students they must sense the *immediacy* of a character's needs. "There must be something dynamic behind the scene," he says. "It's static when there is simply a difference of opinion. Remember, the character must be *fighting to effect change.*"

How does all this affect the writer of a scene in a Soap?

In life few people understand themselves so well that they can articulate, clearly and precisely, what they want or how they're feeling. In our day-to-day living we translate most of our primal needs into something socially acceptable—or more nearly so. The mother who can't bear to lose her son doesn't *say,* "I can't live without you." Instead, she may fairly smother him with small attentions and chicken soup. Or she may casually disparage every girl he goes out with. Or take Alvin Jones the bookkeeper. He may be living a life of quiet desperation, but he would never say, "I am quietly desperate." He might, instead, take up drinking or beating his wife. While neither of those solutions is socially acceptable, you know what I mean. An emotion that is repressed is likely to surface in quite a different form.

The writer must be sharply aware of a character's history, and of the immediate prelude to the scene: what happened to this character before the scene began? And what are the emotions, recognized or not, that underlie the scene? And most important, *what is the character trying to achieve here,* and what does he perceive as a threat to those ends?

Corey has another piece of advice for his actors that a writer also needs to remember: do not give an editorial opinion on the character. Don't make moral judgments. The actor, as the character, must like himself and must feel justified in what he's doing. The writer, too, as he writes a scene, must be inside that character, justifying himself every inch of the way!

Rationalizing one's misdeeds is a common failing. There's no one in the world who doesn't have an excuse for his behavior; no one ever thinks of himself as the villain. Hitler? He operated with total conviction that what he was doing was laudable. The bloodiest wars in history have been holy wars—Hitler "executing" six million Jews, or Christians and Saracens slaughtering each other all through the Middle Ages in the name of the true faith.

Sometimes people knowingly do something wrong but shrive themselves by feeling guilty about it. A sense of guilt makes them feel almost as virtuous as if they hadn't committed the questionable act in the first place. Wonderful stuff, guilt—it has all kinds of uses.

Exercise Your Subtext Sense

But I'm straying away from Corey's advice on subtext. I found, in those classes, that the most effective device he used, to nail the lesson home, was the following exercise. And you might want to try it with a friend.

He paired off his class into couples and asked them each to imagine a two-person conflict situation. Then he distributed at random a number of short, nonexpository scenes from well-known plays. Each couple was to play the scene he'd given them—*using their own invented subtext,* and the scene had to make sense. Every word they said had to relate to the new situation.

Suppose couple A has been handed a portion of the Tracy-Mike scene of Act II scene 2 from *The Philadelphia Story* by Philip Barry. In it the wealthy, beautiful young Tracy Lord is to be married tomorrow to a straitlaced, self-made labor leader-turned-executive. But her attractive former husband has turned up for the prenuptial celebrations, and his presence has shaken her self-confidence. Now, after an all-night party and too much champagne, she's conversing with Mike Connor, an admiring young journalist.

MIKE

Tracy—

TRACY

Yes, Mr. Connor?

MIKE

How do you mean, I'm a "snob"?

TRACY

You're the worst kind there is: an intellectual snob. You've made up your mind awfully young, it seems to me.

MIKE

Thirty's about time to make up your mind. —And I'm nothing of the sort, not Mr. Connor.

TRACY

The time to make up your mind about people is never. Yes you are—and a complete one.

MIKE

You're quite a girl.

TRACY

You think?

MIKE

I know.

TRACY

Thank you, Professor. I don't think I'm exceptional.

MIKE

You are, though.

TRACY

I know any number like me. You ought to get around more.

MIKE

In the Upper Class? No thanks.

TRACY

You're just a mass of prejudices, aren't you? You're so much thought and so little feeling, Professor.

(She moves Right, further away from him.)

That's as much of the scene as we'll use. Let's say that the couple who'll play the scene have, without knowing what scene they'll be given, proposed the following situation:

A man deep in debt has borrowed money from his friends—presumably to pay off what he owes—but instead, he has gone off to Acapulco and spent all the money. Now he's back and is trying to justify himself with his wife who's furious.

Now read those first few lines. The situation is altogether changed. Mike, feeling very much in the wrong, is defending himself by taking the offensive. And Tracy, in this revised version, is filled with righteous anger because she's been through this so often before. The meaning of every line is changed.

Corey's point, in this mix-matching of text and subtext, is to prove that *dialogue is merely an overlay.*

The scenes one chooses for this exercise need to be as unspecific as possible in terms of the play's actual plot. But from there on the possibilities are endless. And for reasons I do not fully understand, such exercises do more to ingrain the need for subtext into the writer's mind than any amount of theory.

I was not the only writer to take advantage of Jeff's subtextual approach. Later on I heard that a number of screenwriters had also sat in on his acting classes: Robert Towne, Bo Goldman, Carol Eastman, Stewart Sterne, Lawrence Hauben. In his chapter in *The Craft of the Screenwriter* (by John Brady) Robert Towne spoke of the same exercise that I have just described and adds: "The acting influenced me as a writer. Watching Jack [Nicholson] improvise really had a great effect. His improvisations were inventive. When he was given a situation he would not improvise on the nose. He'd talk around the problem, and writing is the same way; it's not explicit."

Between Writer and Actor

A certain amount of acting experience is very useful to a Soap writer—not essential, but useful. And it needn't even be professional acting; doing a few plays at the local little theater can help your ear for dialogue enormously. As I've said before, dialogue written and dialogue spoken are vastly different and one needs to learn the distinction early on.

What kinds of lines do actors have trouble with? Here's what some Daytime performers say:

". . . Long speeches which say the same thing four different ways."

". . . If the thought process is askew, or if it's too wordy . . . "

". . . If a transition is too fast. Or if it's something I just can't play . . ."

Or, finally, lines which prompt the actor to say, ruefully, "I don't think the writer could have said this out loud!"

On the other hand, actors who regularly rewrite their lines are not too popular with writers, particularly those actors who change the grammar of a speech. The writer whose line properly reads, "between you and *me*" could sink through the floor when an actor, trying to be elegant, changes it onscreen to "between you and *I*." Most writers are also students of the language and they hate to take the rap for an actor's blunder.

More than grammar is involved in these on-the-set revisions. A writer's intent in a scene is very specific; the dialogue he writes has usually been honed to a fine point, even when it is, as we've just mentioned, overlay. When an actor not attuned to this kind of precision colloquializes a line to make it easier to say, he may unwittingly alter its meaning.

Some Daytime headwriters don't allow such changes. On shows written by William Bell, for instance, the actors are required to be word perfect—not an unmixed blessing because they sometimes find his dialogue a little ornate and hard to read.

Room for complaint can be found on both sides but keep in mind that in Daytime, as in no other entertainment form, the finished product depends on that unacknowledged collaboration between writer and actor. The actor, after all, has been and will be playing this part for years or even decades, and he brings to it a particular style which the writer must learn to write to. In nighttime episodic series the actor is acting; in Daytime he *becomes* the character. Or, more exactly, he and the character become one. The character, with the help of the writer, takes on the actor's speech patterns, rhythm, and attitudes. For example, remember Michael Zaslow as Roger Thorpe in *Guiding Light?* His "sound" was a bitter, mocking irony; if the writer ignored it, Roger's lines didn't work. His dialogue—his whole performance—required that special quality.

Many actors have personality quirks which the perceptive headwriter may incorporate into the story. According to biographer Dan Wakefield, Agnes Nixon sometimes uses her actors' special qualities—as well as their life situations—to enrich the characters they're playing. In the case of one talented, flamboyant actor on *All My Children,* Nixon wrote directly to the man's singing ability and his propensity for flashy clothes. Another actress who had a face-lift provided Nixon with a whole face-lift story line.

Sometimes, too, an actor hired for a one shot—a minor two- or three-day role—takes the part and runs with it. A kind of chemistry takes over; the screen suddenly becomes electric—and the producer and headwriter know they have a winner. Story lines will be altered and scripts rewritten to take advantage of the newcomer, and all of a sudden he's a regular. A classic example is actor Doug Hayes, who was hired for a small background role in a jail scene in *Days of Our Lives,* but he remained by popular acclaim to become one of the show's leads.

On a less spectacular level, even a secondary character's impact can cause story lines to be rewritten. Several years ago actress K.T. Stevens was hired to play a one-shot on *The Young and the Restless*—the part of Vanessa Prentiss, a woman with a badly scarred face which she hid behind a veil. Story plans for Vanessa at that point were uncertain; but the character took off. She was recognized as a valuable heavy, and Stevens stayed with the show for more than five years as the part she played grew steadily more evil, subtly manipulating the lives of the people around her.

When the headwriter finally decided to kill her off, Stevens was given nine months' notice—but even so, she found it surprisingly upsetting. Actors on Daytime come to identify themselves to a great extent with the characters they play, and their fellow actors on the show begin to seem like family. By the same token, a writer who's been with a show for several years also comes to feel closely involved with the characters; and being abruptly fired can feel rather like an amputation without anesthetic.

The Actor and His Character

How long does the melding of character and actor take? Norma Connelly, who plays Ruby on *General Hospital,* says it took her about three months to "become" Ruby. "At that point," she says, "you get it [the part] under lock and key." Other actors say the process can take up to six months.

Let's consider for a moment the importance of the individual actor to the welfare of the show as a whole. What happens when a popular player decides his Daytime job is merely a stepping stone to bigger and better

Pine Valley Gothic: Gillian Spencer, James Mitchell, and Elizabeth Lawrence as Monique (Daisy), Palmer Cortland and Myra Murdoch in All My Children. *ABC photo.*

things, and leaves the show to go to Hollywood? Or let's say his fan mail has been ecstatic and his contract is expiring, and he wants so much money that he prices himself out of the market. What then?

The headwriter—in conjunction with the producer and/or sponsor—has three choices: write him out, kill him off, or replace him. The problem is not unlike that faced by a new headwriter just taking over a show with a batch of preexisting story lines to dispose of. The pros and cons of the first two options were discussed in Chapter Three. How about the third—recasting the part?

That's not an ideal solution either. In fact, it may be the least satisfactory.

When a popular actor is replaced, the credibility of a show is *always* hurt. Daytime viewers are not like film- or play-goers, happy to see their favorite actors tackle anything from *King Lear* to *Arsenic and Old Lace.* To the Daytime viewer the character on a Soap is a *real person;* those situations on the television screen are the stuff of life, and the replacement of an important figure on a show sows confusion, unease, or downright anger in the viewer *who never thought of him as an actor.*

Television historian Robert LaGuardia feels that one of the reasons *Love Is a Many-Splendored Thing* did not survive was the loss (over a salary dispute) of the actor David Birney. It's his opinion that Birney's departure gave the show "an almost mortal wound."

On the other hand, the loss of Eileen Fulton, long a mainstay as Lisa on *As the World Turns,* did not seem to have hurt the program's ratings appreciably—perhaps because, over the last year or two, the importance of her character to the story lines had been imperceptibly downgraded so she was no longer pivotal to the doings in Springfield. This, indeed, may well have been why she chose to leave the show for a time.

A related point is that sometimes, in the current rush for youth oriented material, an actor who has long been identified as one of the core family of a show will, on reaching middle age, find himself reduced to an occasional token appearance or written out altogether. This can only damage the believability of the show and the morale of its players. It's a tragic reflection of the youth worship of our time, and of the uncaring impatience with which older citizens are shunted aside in our society. It's far better for the show to reflect the extended family, old and young, and to deal with an older character's disability or death *within the body of the story line itself*—as happened a decade or two ago on *Guiding Light* when Papa Bauer was allowed to die gently in his sleep as Theo Goetz, the actor who played him, had died. To ignore death and the grieving process is to ignore something that gives meaning and dignity to life; a Daytime show cheats its audience if death is treated only as a melodramatic device.

Similarly, the premature and tragically sudden death of actress Melba Rae, who played Marge Bergman on *Search for Tomorrow,* was dealt with as a fact on the show as well; loss and grief were handled with exquisite taste by both writers and actors, providing scenes of extraordinary tenderness which gave the show a stature it has not attained since. For example, when Marge's widowed husband, Stu—played by Larry Haines—in his loneliness got a crush on a young schoolteacher some six months later, fans wrote letters by the truckload. They could not bear to see their beloved Stu make a fool of himself over a younger woman.

In this context of a show's realism and believability, let's touch on one aberration that arises from time to time to plague headwriters: the guest appearance—a device usually decided on by the sponsor or producer when the show's ratings need an extra boost. Whatever the theory behind it, the net effect is to jolt the viewer out of a sense that the show is really happening and to remind him that it is, after all, just show biz.

1981 and 1982 were big years for cameo appearances; shows vied with each other to see which one could bag the biggest Hollywood name. Headwriters struggled to assimilate these trophies into the fabric of the story, but for two or three appearances, it was hardly worth it, and the show's most valuable commodity—its credibility—invariably suffered. Fortunately, Procter & Gamble has decided that names, when not integral to the story, do *not* improve the ratings.

The operative phrase here is, of course, "integral to the story." Mrs. Cassidine, the character played by Elizabeth Taylor in *General Hospital, was* integrated into the story, and she was considered a substantial plus. The five episodes in which she appeared, by the way, were shot in a breakneck two days, and the star won the respect of all her fellow actors with her competence and professionalism. Sammy Davis, Jr. also spent five weeks on the show in a major role, and he too was considered a valuable addition. In Taylor's case, her appearance boosted the ratings by a full point— almost an embarrassment of riches since the show at that time was already cruising at the top of the ratings chart.

Credit Where It's Due

I have a natural prejudice in favor of the importance of the writer's contribution to the finished product; writers in film and television lead an uphill battle for recognition at the best of times. Ours is an industry where the widely

Three's a crowd on **The Young and the Restless.** *Lilibet Stern as Patty Williams, Terry Lester as Jack Abbott, and Alex Donnelley as Diane Jenkins. CBS photo.*

prevalent *auteur* theory tends to give the director credit for everything on the screen from story to special effects. And fans seem to think the actors speak their lines spontaneously. So when I talk about actors, let's not lose sight of those hours the Daytime writer has spent at his typewriter, fine-tuning those scenes.

But let's also remind ourselves of the substantial contribution made by many Daytime actors.

Members of the trade agree that working in Daytime is the most difficult and demanding kind of acting there is. A Soap actor has less time to learn his script than in any other field; his hours are longer by far; and the work, when he's a regular, is ceaseless. He also has too little rehearsal time. And yet, day after day, remarkable performances appear on the screen.

There are also many inadequate performances. Daytime is filled with pretty, faceless young men and women who are all but interchangeable. But if they stay in Daytime, *some* of them may learn their craft and become, finally, real actors. As a training ground, soap opera has no equal; it is the present-day substitute for barnstorming and repertory theater. Additionally, since the camera is close and relentless, there's no room for "ham" on Daytime; a conscientious young actor is forced to learn subtlety, shading—and subtext.

The training tells. And sometime down the road, a part will come along which the young actor will make truly his own, and another dimension will be added to the show.

And so, without depreciating the writer's contribution, let's give a salute to the actors who spend fifty or fifty-two weeks a year, twelve or fourteen hours a day, creating (with help from the typewritten page) living, breathing human beings. They deserve every bit of appreciation and respect we can give them.

12

The Raw Material

Until now we have dealt with the technical aspect of writing for Soaps; how it happens, how it's done. But just as a cake isn't a cake without flour, baking powder, eggs, milk, and flavoring, there are certain basic ingredients to a good daytime drama without which we'd end up pulling another kind of article altogether out of the oven.

What are they? When our headwriter sits down to create a soap opera what are the ingredients that this new bible must contain? What, in other words, do all Daytime dramas have in common?

Most important, there is at least one core family.

The core family (and the larger it is, the more story lines it will provide) will be at the center of all the bible's main events. Other stories may spin off from it. Outside characters may affect or be affected by its members, but the welfare and survival of this central family is what provides the basic structure of a good daytime drama. The core family is the family we wish we were part of. They are *us.*

Well, if not exactly us, they are us as we would wish to be, or as we see ourselves. That means they should in most cases be middle-class, give or take a notch. On a few shows, the core family is upper-middle-class or even rich (like the Forbes family in *Loving,* the Stewarts in *As the World Turns*), satisfying our need for wish fulfillment—but it's dangerous to make them poor. The audience doesn't like to watch people poorer than themselves. It makes them anxious; these are not lives they want to share or even know much about. Poverty does not make good soap opera. While viewers may be upwardly mobile in terms of the characters they identify with, they are not downwardly mobile.

A major exception is *Ryan's Hope,* a show that came into being with a lower-middle-class family at its center. How did the writers manage to pull it off? There were compensations. Johnny and Maeve Ryan and their children were so warm, so loving and supportive of each other, that we the viewers felt we could safely enter into their world even if they *didn't* have any money. They had enough emotional wealth in other words to make up for their lack of financial security. Remember what Paul Avila Mayer said: "The Ryans were the family I wished I had grown up with."

Also they had the wealthy Coleridge family as their friends and later marriage partners. In time the Coleridges came to constitute a secondary core.

Most Soaps have secondary or even tertiary core families whose function, often, is to provide contrast or conflict with the primary family. *Capitol,* for instance, began its life with three such clans: The McCandlesses (the family we care most about), the Cleggs (about whom we have very mixed feelings), and the Dennings, with the dangerous Paula playing at being agoraphobic and causing trouble for everyone. Rich in backstory, this show gets much of its drive from the bitterness, born of ancient wrongs, that these families feel for each other—antagonisms so powerful that the show at times seems almost self-propelling. *Capitol* is a marvel of backstory.

Extended Families

What other factors help us as we populate a new show? I'm speaking here in the most simplistic terms, describing the characters in terms of their structural function on the show and the plot purposes they serve. It's up to the writer to turn these chess pieces into living, breathing, idiosyncratic human beings. What kinds of people give us the variety and the story potential we need?

For one thing, it helps if the core family is multigenerational. This gives us a wide age range of characters for the audience to identify with. Additionally, a grandparent can function as a source of wisdom on the show, rather like a prophet or village sage. Frank and Doris Hursley used to say that such a character made the viewer himself feel wise. As I've mentioned before, the swing toward youth-oriented stories has displaced a lot of these voice-of-wisdom oldsters, but a few survive, and they give a show a feeling of richness and continuity.

More essential, however, are family members who are "franchise" characters—people like doctors, lawyers, judges, and policemen, who by virtue of their occupations have a *franchise* to involve themselves authoritatively in other people's lives. The arenas in which they operate provide a wealth of story material, as well as all that lovely local color. ("The prosecution rests, your Honor," "Did you read the prisoner his rights?" and "We have a hot appendix in Room 543.")

Of course a show needs young people. I know I've complained about the extent to which these unfledged nestlings have come to dominate the Daytime screen. But we do need them for several reasons. Once involved, a teenage viewer may continue to watch the show for decades—a matter of considerable interest to the sponsor. Also a story of star-crossed young love, a good Romeo and Juliet story, is hard to beat no matter what its current transmogrification. At the soap opera convention mentioned earlier, panelists agreed that this was one of the most durable of all story lines; once under way, it can go on indefinitely. But as soon as the lovers get together, it's all over, a problem we'll get to shortly.

Let's double back briefly. I should have mentioned, when I was talking about the core family, that the individual members of this family will be our protagonists: the characters we care about, feel for, weep with, whose joys and tribulations we share. The need for characters to love is so basic and so obvious I hate to bring it up—like insisting the sky is blue. But let's speak of them now just to make sure they are front and center when our story begins. The lives of these characters are the other lives we live; they parallel our own.

Conversely, every show must provide us with at least one character we love to hate. From the time of Cain we have peopled our legends with villains. A good villain is absolutely essential to a daytime drama, and sometimes he becomes its very backbone. We'll tune in week after week just to see what new outrage he's committing now. I'm not sure why his villainy is so intriguing to us. Perhaps it's because of the suspense he provides as he puts our heroes and heroines in continual jeopardy. Or perhaps he is, in some curious way, a personification of all those selfish, antisocial impulses within ourselves that we don't dare act on but so often want to. Or perhaps we all carry within us a reservoir of free-floating, unexpressed hostility that needs letting out. Whatever the reason, at least one good rousing heavy is indispensable to a satisfactory Soap. Two are even better.

Keep in mind, however, that just as our sympathetic characters are more believable if they are slightly flawed (like Ed Bauer and his alcoholism in *Guiding Light*), a heavy is more credible if he has a few redeeming features. Think of John Dixon on *As the World Turns,* for instance—one of the most gloriously successful heavies on Daytime. He is a man guilty of one offense after another against all the characters we love most—and yet we un-

149

A clutch of Donovans in Loving: *James Kiberd, Lauren Marie Taylor, and Bryan Cranston as Mike, Stacey, and Douglas. ABC photo.*

derstand him. We almost sympathize with him. He is unloved, and knows himself unloved, and for this our hearts bleed for him, a fallen Lucifer. Sometimes we think he's on the verge of rehabilitation, but it never quite happens. John Dixon's lonely villainy is the glue that holds his show together.

The Best-Laid Plans . . .

The imponderable in all this is what audience reaction to any character, protagonist or heavy, will be. That depends, as often as not, on the actor playing the part. Also, sometimes a story line that looks wonderful on paper will, on the screen, fall on its face—just as another story line will, for reasons equally obscure, take off.

For example, Paul Avila Mayer reports that the bible of *Ryan's Hope* was originally about two hundred pages long: the first half dealing with some sixteen major characters, and the second half projecting about two years of story lines. But six weeks into production, he says, the second half was thrown out (presumably because the story lines weren't working). The best-laid plans of mice, men and headwriters . . .

In any event, the bible must above all offer stories that will provide and maintain suspense. Happy endings, within the body of the story projection, must be avoided—as they must be avoided down the road when other headwriters take over the show.

Why should this be when so much of a show's fan mail *begs* the producer to let John and Mary get together and be happy? Don't the fans know what they want?

In this instance, no.

In soap opera as in life, there may be moments of respite—moments at least long enough to let characters get a better grip on the life preserver. But these moments can't last long because—alas for the course of true love—fulfillment and happiness are *undramatic.* The mortality rate for happy marriages on Daytime is hair-raising. An associate writer finds himself writing "Dearly beloved, we are gathered together" so often he almost knows the whole ceremony by heart. But the happy couple he is marrying had better take a good look at each other; one of them may not be around very long. Why do you think poor Dan Hughes acquired a fatal illness on *As the World Turns* several years ago? It was because his marriage to Kim was so happy there was no place for the story to go. The same fans, in other words, who urge a show's producer to bring a long-running romance to consummation will stop watching it when it actually happens. No more suspense!

There's one other factor that Daytime drama needs: a touch of comedy, and the bible ought to include a character or characters who can provide it. I'm not talking about comic characters extraneous to the central story (as, if you'll forgive me, I think many of Shakespeare's clowns are), but people intrinsic to it. When the viewer has been at a high point of tension for most of the show's half-hour or hour running time, he is unutterably grateful for a few laughs. Even when we are not dealing with characters who are themselves comic, we should remember that American speech patterns are for the most part wry, dry, and droll. Associate writers should listen to supermarket clerks, bus drivers—even high school students. Their most casual comment is usually *funny.* The single quality I find most enchanting about my countrymen is that they rarely take themselves, or anyone else, too seriously. A show's dialogue should reflect that.

Some Thoughts from Agnes Nixon

Before we leave the subject of the necessary ingredients of a bible and move to the matter of day-to-day content, let's pause to consider the record of the *doyenne* of all soap opera, Agnes Nixon—the creator and headwriter of more successful daytime drama than any other living writer. One can't look over her list of hits without wondering how in the world one writer can keep hitting home runs with such astonishing accuracy. In pursuit of an answer, even a partial answer, I wrote her, asking for an interview on the subject. Under the relentless time pressure of keeping watch over not one but *two* current shows, she agreed instead to answer a few written questions.

Here are some of the results of that interview:

> *QUESTION:* Beyond the bare bones of one or two "core" families, and the essential protagonists and heavy or heavies (and someone to provide a little comedy?)—are there particular *kinds* of characters you feel are needed to round out a full and satisfying story?
>
> *ANSWER:* No. Simply characters who fit in well with the others and are contemporary, presenting a picture of today's society in some form.
>
> *QUESTION:* The (show's) locale: is this necessarily a "wish-fulfillment" sort of place, one we all wished we lived in, or do you feel it should have other uses?
>
> *ANSWER:* I don't feel it a "wish-fulfillment" locale in any sense, at least that has never been my intention. I feel it should again be a place where believable stories can occur and reflect modern-day life.
>
> *QUESTION:* Do you usually have a thesis or a theme in mind when you create a show?
>
> *ANSWER:* In a very general sense there is a thesis or theme. For *All My Children* it was the brotherhood of man and for *Loving* it is that love is needed by all mankind and without it we cannot be in any sense a contented person.
>
> *QUESTION:* Have you found any conflict between a show's relevance—and its universality?
>
> *ANSWER:* No. It only needs time and thought to tell the story in a relevant, universal way.
>
> *QUESTION:* —Or between the pace of a show and the amount of depth you're able to give it?

ANSWER: Because we do 260 episodes a year we have the time—which is what I suppose you mean by "pace"—to do any story in depth.

QUESTION: Several headwriters have said, in effect, "We have a mandate to entertain." Your shows have shown a good deal more profundity than that, often dealing with important sociological issues. Have you ever met with viewer resistance to a particular subject—enough to require changing a story line? Have you ever found it difficult to find a mean between entertainment and content?

ANSWER: When one is doing issues of social relevance, often with controversy inherent in them, inevitably with eleven million viewers a day some will not like the story so much as others. Some will object to the subject matter. But as time goes on and one is able to explore the story and explain why a person is a certain way we have found that the stories are accepted by the viewers and there is not a conflict between entertainment and content.

QUESTION: What do you feel are the most important factors to be included in a successful bible?

ANSWER: Since I have never asked myself what the most important factors are to be included in a successful bible this is a very difficult question to answer. I suppose one could say believable interesting characters in relevant suspenseful plots and overall stories.

QUESTION: And do you feel a creator's continuing involvement with his show, even after another headwriter takes over the plotting, is important to its survival? To what extent do you try to provide continued guidance to the shows you have created?

ANSWER: Whether a creator even has a continuing involvement with any show after another headwriter takes over is dependent on the network which is at that point producing the show and if that network wants the creator to continue having an involvement, in a consultancy capacity or story analyst, whatever one wishes to call it. The final part of that question is simply that I try to provide guidance if guidance is needed. I could not possibly give you any set answer in terms of quantity, quality, length of time, etc.

NBC's new Santa Barbara *brings youth, sex, and an expensive look to the Daytime scene. Above, Robin Wright as Kelly Capwell and Steve Meadows as Peter Flint try a romantic weekend. NBC photo.*

There is enough substance in the above answers to keep us busy discussing them for quite a while. But if, in my questions, I was looking for a magic word, a touchstone, a fail-safe formula to pass along to the would-be Daytime writer, it was a foolish quest, not possible of fulfillment. Ms. Nixon's answers are direct and to the point, they can help us in a general sense. But I realize now the two most important factors in the success of her shows cannot really be communicated to even the most eager student of the form— her lifetime experience at the craft and her remarkable understanding of the scene she's writing about. She knows us, in other words, better than we know ourselves.

Taboos, Fads, Gimmicks

With a single exception, I won't go into the matter of locale; the headwriter must decide whether an urban, suburban, or small-town setting serves his purpose best. However, it's interesting in view of *Loving's* general acceptance to note that a decade or two ago there was a rule of thumb among Daytime executives that a college background was poison; that it would merely aggravate an already prevalent anti-intellectual bias on the part of the viewer. *Bright Promise,* created by the Hursleys in 1969, tried to fly in the face of this prejudice, and whether the bias did in fact exist or the networks merely *thought* it did, the show went through a series of headwriters, lasted a couple of years, and died. Now, however, we have *Loving* placed against a college background, defying not only the anticollege bias but several others besides, and it seems to be doing nicely.

Times change, or perhaps viewers do.

Leaving the bible for a moment, let's consider the problem of content for an ongoing show. In his *Eight Years in Another World,* Harding Lemay gives us a clear-eyed look at the dilemma faced by many a conscientious headwriter. Initially, he says, "I did not expect the freedom to write anything I chose, as I enjoyed when writing a play or book, but I resolved to write honestly about how people live and love, marry and die." Later in the book he remarks, with understandable pride, "I had survived two years of writing a soap opera without resorting to murder, amnesia, an illegitimate baby, sudden surgery, or courtroom scenes. The story lines were based on interaction between ambivalent characters, whose aspirations were often at war with their intrinsic natures."

Again, the best-laid plans . . . As time went on, so did the pressure, and finally, little by little, he bowed to it and began introducing into his show many of the melodramatic devices he had struggled so long to avoid. Although ratings were high, his own relationship to the material was badly damaged. "Once having violated the essential natures of the characters I had created with great care," he writes, "I did not regain pristine faith in them. The fans and sponsors may have been pleased by what I wrote, but I was ashamed of it."

There are fads in Daytime, often urged upon the headwriter by the sponsor or network in the belief that such-and-such a gimmick will stimulate the ratings. Even more destructive than the hyped-up melodrama Lemay tried so hard to avoid was the science-fiction jag so many of the Daytime shows embarked on in 1981 and 1982. Mad scientists who wanted to rule the world and homicidal, maniacal dwarfs . . . such vagaries may have appealed to the *Star Wars* addicts in the audience and to college students who enjoyed them as camp—but how about the show's long-range (sometimes lifelong) viewers to whom the show's regular characters were not actors but old friends and real people? How about that absolutely essential ingredient in successful soap opera—credibility? And how long will it take, now that the fad is over, to reestablish that credibility?

A headwriter faces other philosophic choices. What about the inclusion of black characters and black story lines? We live, after all, in a multicultural, multiracial society, and to ignore the presence of minorities in that society is to ignore what's been happening in America since the civil rights movement began. On the other hand, though we pay a good deal of lip service to the principles of equal opportunity, we are not yet wholly or truly integrated. And since the requisite for a good story projection is that its various story lines be intertwined, what to do? How can our black-white story lines be integrated when our society is, to an unhappy extent, still segregated?

Luckily for the Daytime writer, affirmative action programs have guaranteed that minority doctors, lawyers, policemen, and teachers (among others) must now be represented on hospital staffs, in law offices and courtrooms, in station houses, and on college faculties. And the entertainment world has always been color-blind to a certain extent. So in these institutions at least, Daytime characters of various racial and cultural backgrounds can meet and get involved with each other. In the last year or two there have been strong black stories on *One Life to Live, Another World, As the World Turns,* and *All My Children,* and there may be others by the time this book goes to press. These are all one-hour shows. For a half-hour show, with only half as many story lines, it's more difficult; perhaps the conventional wisdom is that national demographics don't justify using one-third of a show's daily air-time on stories that may have special appeal to only 11 percent of the population.

This raises another question: do minority viewers necessarily identify more with minority story lines, or doesn't it matter? My feeling is that it doesn't. For years, black audiences watched soap opera when there were no black stories. And I can't believe that white audiences don't identify totally with the problems of Jesse and Angie and their baby on *All My Children*. After all, a good story is a good story is a good story. And perhaps some day none of these differences will be a factor in our Daytime preferences, and soap opera will have come truly to represent the diversity and cultural richness of our entire society.

Controversy—and Responsibility

How about controversial subject matter generally? What is the attitude of sponsors and networks toward abortion, for instance, on soap opera?

The question arose a few years ago on *Search for Tomorrow*. Procter & Gamble, with commendable restraint, asked only that the headwriter present both sides of the issue—not editorially of course but dramatically. This continues to be the position of most executives in a decision-making capacity. Let's hear a few comments from the panelists at that Daytime convention:

"We can't satisfy every pressure group. But we do try to deal with some."

"We don't pick an issue and put it on the show. We write character and story."

"The writer must present both sides, and it must involve relationships."

"The need is to entertain as many people as possible; we're not here to improve them."

In all cases, it was agreed, the handling of controversial material *must be governed by good taste.*

At the time of that convention in early 1983, there were still certain subjects Daytime strove to avoid: homosexuality, miscegenation, heavy drug stories, incest, child abuse—and for reasons I'll get to shortly, suicide. But in the intervening months, what has happened? Taboos have come crashing down on two Agnes Nixon shows: Garth Slater's advances have driven his daughter into schizophrenia on *Loving;* and on *All My Children,* a warm, sympathetic young woman psychologist tells another character, "I'm gay."

Let's take up *Loving* first. Nixon and Doug Marland have said, in ef-

157

fect, that the tragedy of incest and child abuse can occur even among the most respectable members of society, with a devastating effect on the victim. The story line was almost a prophetic forerunner of the controversy now swirling around the publication of Freud's recently revealed early correspondence about childhood seduction.

As for *All My Children*—after Lynn's frank admission to her friend Devon, we learned her backstory; what the recognition of her sexual orientation meant to her, and what difficulties can ensue for a gay person in a mostly straight world. The material was dealt with emphathically and with consummate good taste—even with a little comedy as Devon tried frantically to appear broad-minded on the subject. Of all current writers Nixon is doing the most to create understanding and a sense of common humanity between black and white, straight and gay, and in so doing, is helping Daytime meet its larger obligations.

Suicide is another area in which Daytime writers and executives take an impressively responsible position. They recognize that an unstable viewer may be swayed by what he sees on the television screen, and may, in fact, choose to emulate the action of even an unsympathetic character. *No one involved in Daytime wants to give the audience the idea that suicide is a solution to anything.*

And in those rare instances when this injunction is violated, the results are as feared. A sociologist at the University of California, San Diego, researching the effect of television violence and suicide on the behavior of the population as a whole, found a direct correlation. Suicides on televised soap operas, he reported, were generally followed by an increase in the national suicide rate.

It's not a responsibility to be ignored.

And now, perhaps we should move on to a careful examination of the tools and training a Daytime writer needs to ply his trade. After that we'll take up the matter of the economic structure of Daytime because economics are the ultimate reality of the form. But first let's consider the nitty-gritty of actually *becoming* a Daytime writer. How difficult is it? Can anyone do it? Are there any particular qualifications one needs, any special requirements? Or can one simply sit down and do it as Grandma Moses, (I suppose) simply picked up a paintbrush and started painting?

Read on and find out.

13

The Craft So Long to Lerne

At the outset, let's get rid of that Grandma Moses analogy. She was a primitive, and to my knowledge no writer has ever made it as a primitive. Among nonwriters, however, there seems to be a widespread misconception that *any*one can write. It's just a matter, the logic goes, of putting down one's thoughts on paper—isn't it?

No.

There is a vast difference between spoken and written English. All writing demands precision, clarity, and a sense of the rhythm of a line. It also requires a certain knowledge of the literature of one's own and other fields—and in addition, for both playwriting and screenwriting, some knowledge of the basic tenets of dramatic structure. A Daytime writer doesn't need a Ph.D. (though you'd be surprised at the number who have them), but he must have a facility with the language; that's the tool without which he can't function at all.

In fact two kinds of equipment are vital: the abstract kind, like those I've just mentioned, and the physical tools it takes simply to get a readable scene down on paper. Let's take a look first at those, since they're more easily acquired, and get back to the literary requirements later.

First of all, a writer needs a typewriter—preferably one with pica type, because elite throws off the pagination and is harder to read. Any type that calls attention to itself and interposes itself between the writer and the reader—like the kind that imitates script—is a minus, not a plus. The headwriter must read hundreds of pages a week, so give him a break: use good, clear, simple, open typeface.

There is a current move among writers toward using word processors. Judging from the conversations around the Writers Guild, you'd think there was an absolute correlation between a state-of-the-art processor and the literary material that comes out of it. That's as may be. Certainly, as an electronics illiterate who's never even been able to master a typewriter without a moveable carriage, this writer doesn't think she's a candidate for any such brave new world. Also, remember that while Dickens was turning out those tens of thousands of pages, he relied on an obliging sister-in-law to make a "fair copy" for his publishers. Tolstoi's wife did the same—at least as long as they were on speaking terms. So let other adventurous souls cope with their floppy discs; give me a good sturdy office-model electric, with a portable on hand for emergencies, and Wilderness is Paradise enow."

The Writer's Home Library

So much for typewriters. Once our writer gets a job, there are certain books he'll need on his shelf for instant research, so he doesn't have to waste precious time rushing off to the reference desk of the public library. Among them should be a good dictionary; a *Roget's Thesaurus* (do you know that W.C. Fields used a thesaurus when he was fine-tooling some of those wonderful comedy scenes in his movies?); a *Bartlett's Quotations;* a recent world almanac; perhaps a book on English usage like Strunk and White's *The Elements of Style;* and, near his typewriter, one of those word books that doesn't bother with definitions but simply gives the spelling. Webster has one in paperback that I find indispensable. (There's a word I *always* have to look up: is it *-ible* or *-able?*)

But why, you may ask, is spelling so important? Anyone with half a brain ought to know what we mean.

Not so. Like grammatical errors, a misspelling that crops up in the middle of a scene can stop the reader cold—and the reader in this case is probably the headwriter. Such an error interrupts his flow of thought and magnifies itself out of all proportion. It's as though the associate writer had gone out for a job interview in mismatched socks; it shouldn't be important, but it is. Therefore, if you don't want to offend your headwriter's sensibilities, be sure of your spelling and grammar—and, while you're about it, the precise meaning of the words you use.

How about an encyclopedia? I have one but use it infrequently; perhaps that's something you *can* leave to your local library. A reference source you'll use far more frequently is the *Merck Manual,* with a one-volume medical encyclopedia to translate those technical terms. I often think that "subdural hemotoma" is the most used phrase in Daytime drama.

Even with those two aids, however, you'll need to supplement your information with a call to your doctor to make sure your medical dialogue is both accurate and colloquial. But it takes a certain minimal understanding of illness or wounds or treatment before you even know what to *ask* a doctor, and that's where the *Merck Manual* proves useful.

The same is true of law handbooks. You may find yourself having to give two of your attorney characters some throw-away dialogue at the opening of a scene, or you may be dealing with an arrest where the arresting officer must read the Miranda rights to the culprit. Or perhaps the story line takes you into a complicated courtroom scene, in which case you'll need all the technical help you can get. So you may need several such handbooks, including a glossary of legal terms and books dealing with both civil and criminal law. (I just counted mine. I have *seven.*) And even these will merely provide a startling point; you will *still* need to phone an attorney and, if there's time, head for the local courthouse so you'll know what the set ought to look like and what functions the bailiff, the clerk, and the court stenographer serve.

Now that Daytime is taking its characters on location, you'll need not only a recent atlas but one or two good travel books, and several language dictionaries. (Thus far I've had to write lines of dialogue in Spanish, French, Swedish, Italian, and Greek.) And if your character speaks more than a word or two in his native tongue, you'd better bypass those dictionaries and phone a consulate or an airline of whichever country you're dealing with to get a colloquial translation and to be sure the syntax is accurate. Cultural attachés are helpful, as are people in the language department of the local university. The Greek used in that scene from *As the World Turns,* by the way, was provided by an unemployed Greek actress the people in my Xerox office happened to know!

Some story lines require expertise in more areas than one writer can possibly be prepared for—and in those troublesome emergencies, just hope you're not writing on a day when your library or other informational center is closed. That's the most difficult part of having to write on Sundays.

While we're on the subject of expertise, what *are* some of those esoteric, or even not so esoteric, fields an associate may be required to become an instant expert in? Here is a tiny fraction of the subjects I've had to research for Daytime shows:

Police academy training. The use of restraints in public mental hospitals. No-fault divorce (which states have it and which don't). Subdural hematoma. Eighteenth-century British speech and social customs. Braille institutes. Egyptian dynasties. The surgical scrub and O.R. procedure. Polygraphs. How to say "Fasten your seat belts" in Greek. Ciphers, EBCDIC, ASCII, and the hexadecimal system (that was a tough script). Silver mining. Immune suppressives. Graphics. Cardiopulmonary resuscitation and para-medic procedures. "Outside the scope" and "Leading the witness." Land-ing an airplane without previous flight training. Kidney transplant. Proce-dures for marriage in France, and the wording (in French) of the ceremony.

This reminds me: you'll need a copy of the Book of Common Prayer and one of the Presbyterian marriage service (revised). You'll also need a copy of a typical civil marriage ceremony. And as a logical next step, you'll need something on childbirth. I've had to write a whole one-hour script de-tailing an emergency home delivery by the Lamaze method—minute by minute, onscreen, although of necessity much of the action took place be-low frame. (You'll be glad to know that both mother and child were fine.)

In other words, anything and everything is grist to the headwriter's mill, and you'd better be prepared. But we're not through yet. There's still more.

Since the daily newspaper and a weekly news magazine frequently provide the headwriter with story ideas, you should keep current with what's going on in the world. A couple of years ago almost half of the Soaps on the air had story lines about surrogate motherhood. That came right out of the headlines. The news also provides stories about runaways, the drug scene, free clinics, political scandals, embezzlement, murder, domestic violence, and a thousand other aspects of life we may have had no personal experi-ence of. So keep abreast. It can only help.

The Learning Ground

This brings us to the other kinds of reading our associate writer needs to have done, the fields of general knowledge he needs to be able to draw on for the fulfillment of his writing tasks.

Earlier in this chapter I mentioned "the rhythm of a line." Every kind of writing—narrative, nonfiction, dramatic—has such a rhythm, or should have. The most famous prose example is the Gettysburg Address. *Moby Dick* is no slouch either, and the King James Version of the Bible is a prime example. Take another look at them; there is an almost oceanic roll to all three. Any writer, in any field, needs to develop an ear for such rhythms. And the best way I know to develop an ear is through poetry—writing it and read-ing it.

Poetry and soap opera? Isn't there a slight contradiction in terms here?

That depends on the Soap. Check back to the quotes from that soap opera convention mentioned in Chapter Six. One headwriter spoke of a couple of his scriptwriters as "poets." Another spoke of associate writing as "almost an art." A director mentioned "the moment that sings." Daytime drama can be plodding and pedestrian or it can be as finely tooled, as finely crafted and written, as any play on Broadway. I don't mean grandiose. But I do mean that Daytime dialogue needs to be written with a feeling for all the music, rhythm, and imagery possible in ordinary human speech. These qualities should be so deeply ingrained in the writer's repertoire that he is almost unconscious of their presence, but they need to be there.

And poetry is the learning ground. I've never polled my writer friends, but I'll bet my bottom dollar that when they were in their mid- to late teens, 90 percent were in their rooms struggling with iambic pentameter or free verse—also good training, Robert Frost notwithstanding. They may have outgrown the affliction, or they may still be closet poets, but the experience will have had its effect; the ear will have become attuned. Also, adolescent poetry is diagnostic; it may be the first indication of a future lifelong love affair with words.

In addition, our writer-to-be needs to familiarize himself with current plays and films. Because styles in dramatic writing change. A movie of forty years ago now seems unconscionably wordy. Everything was *said,* nothing *implied.* Modern dramatic writers have learned the art of indirection. Clifford Odets' exciting agitprop plays of the Depression now seem as outdated as Arthur Wing Pinero's drawing-room comedies of the turn of the century.

Reading for Insight

As he writes, our associate writer finds himself drawing, either consciously or unconsciously, on a wide variety of material he's read during his lifetime. He needs, for instance, at least a speaking acquaintance with elementary psychology and human development. He doesn't need to have read Freud—it might be better if he hasn't—but he does need a sense of the kinds of fixations Freud pinpointed, and the probable reasons for them. As an example, consider *Loving's* aforementioned storyline about incest and child abuse. Or perhaps our writer has to write about a sociopath, or more specifically, a congenital liar. There is a whole machinery involved in an infant's lack of a caring adult at a crucial stage of development that can affect the formation of his conscience. Our writer may not have to deal with the character's backstory, but he's on much firmer ground if he's aware of the forces that produce such a person. A sociopath doesn't just happen; he's

Not as wicked as they seemed: **General Hospital's** *Emma Samms as Holly Sutton, and Tristan Rogers as Robert Scorpio—two who began as villains but emerged on the side of the angels. ABC photo.*

like that for a reason, and if our writer wants to drop a few throwaway lines of dialogue about the character's childhood, it's far better if they are psychologically accurate.

Don't get me wrong; I'm not advocating psychoanalysis as the *deus ex machina* in any piece of dramatic writing. A writer's job is to present the problem, not the simplistic solution. One needs to think of one's characters as individuals who are completely idiosyncratic, not case histories. The same holds for sociological solutions. Yes, it is damaging for a child to be raised in a slum, but all slum children are not therefore alike. To quote a Burl Ives song, every little soul must shine. Psychoanalysis or slum clearance may solve some of the problems but not all of them. Think of the old masters—what if they'd drawn nothing but skeletons and musculature? As a painter needs to know anatomy but conceals it beneath the flesh and the clothing, a writer needs to understand (but not be too mechanical about) the dynamics of human behavior.

A fairly substantial background in reading fiction is useful, too. When an associate is pounding out fifteen or twenty pages a day, it helps to be able to reach into the scrap-bag of his fondest literary memories and pull out the pattern for a given scene as it was handled by, let's say, Dickens when his characters were in a similar situation.

How does it work, this business of going back to our literary models? Well, several years ago one of the Dobsons' outlines for *Guiding Light* called for the self-hating black sheep Roger Thorpe to propose to the virtuous Peggy Fletcher. The trouble was Roger would have known that with his scandal-ridden background, he wouldn't stand a chance with Peggy. He was also perceptive enough to know he didn't in any way deserve a girl like that. How to handle the scene?

I found my pattern in a scene in *A Tale of Two Cities,* which I'd always wept over when I read it to my children: Sydney Carton's self-deprecatory pledge of love and loyalty to Lucy Manette. It is the avowal of the hopeless suitor who wants only to be allowed to be useful in any small way to the woman he loves.

It worked.

And the imagery Dickens used in *Dombey and Son* to describe the death of little Paul Dombey ("Now the boat was out at sea, but gliding smoothly on. And now, there was a shore before him. Who stood on the bank!—") gave me the clue to Nick Andropoulos's dying line in the scene you read earlier from *As the World Turns.*

We're not talking about literary theft. We're talking about gaining insights we might not otherwise have into recurring human predicaments.

Gilbert Murray says, "It is one of the very feeblest critical errors to suppose that there is such a thing called 'originality,' which consists in having no models." Murray was setting up another hypothesis, an important one which we'll get to—but on a more immediate level he seems to be telling us that there is nothing new under the sun, and we needn't worry about it. Our predecessors have all been there already.

The Deep Roots of Storytelling

In this regard, it's also helpful for an associate writer to be conversant with myths and archetypes, and if you don't want to read Jung (I never have), I recommend Murray's *The Classical Tradition in Poetry* and Ernest Jones' *Hamlet and Oedipus.* Listen to Murray (who translated, magnificently, most of the Greek dramatists), and then we can apply what he says to Daytime writing:

Myths, he says, were never invented in a vacuum. "An element drawn from real life was there, no doubt, even at the beginning." He speaks of subjects that "particularly stirred the interests of primitive men [which] still have an appeal to certain very deep-rooted human instincts." They are, he suggests, "deeply implanted in the memory of the race, stamped, as it were, upon our physical organism. We have forgotten their faces and their voices; we say that they are strange to us. *Yet there is that within us which leaps at the sight of them, a cry of the blood which tells us we have known them always.*" (Italics mine.)

It was Ernest Jones to whom Laurence Olivier went when he was preparing his *Hamlet* for the Old Vic; like any good actor he was trying to find out what made the character tick. Jones, a student and biographer of Freud, had just done a study of the relationship between the Hamlet and Oedipus stories. Those who saw Olivier's subsequent film of *Hamlet* may have been aware of Jones' contribution to the performance: it was a profound and moving interpretation of a young man paralyzed by an unresolved Oedipal complex.

While the Hamlet story had been around for centuries, with Iranian, Norse, and Irish versions—even an English dramatization (probably by Thomas Kyd) playing in London ten years before Shakespeare's version—why was it Shakespeare's that caught the popular imagination, and still does?

Jones says, "There is . . . reason to believe that the new life which Shakespeare poured into the old story was the outcome of inspirations that took their original in the deepest and darkest regions of his mind . . . It is only fitting that the greatest work of the world-poet should have to do with the deepest problem and the intensest conflict that have occupied the mind of man since the beginning of time—the revolt of youth and of the impulse to love against the restraint imposed by the jealous eld."

From the point of view of the Daytime writer, myths are not only an unending source of material; they give depth and understanding to most of the conflicts inherent in the human condition.

Before we leave this subject, let's return to Gilbert Murray. He speaks of the richness of the characters, the story, the poets' and dramatists' skills "(i)n plays like *Hamlet* or the *Agamemnon* or the *Electra* . . . but we have, also, I suspect, a strange unanalyzed vibration below the surface, an undercurrent of desires and fears and passions, long slumbering yet eternally familiar, which have for thousands of years lain near the root of our most intimate emotions and been wrought into the fabric of our most magical dreams."

That, it seems to me, is what storytelling is all about.

Granting the truth of all the foregoing, however, we must still come back to what I referred to as "the ultimate reality" of soap opera—its economic structure. This is the determining factor in Daytime's very existence, and a headwriter ignores it to his peril. Although a network will usually give a new show about two years to establish itself, after that it must sink or swim.

This is not necessarily true on prime time. Sometimes a devoted executive will keep a nighttime show going for its prestige value in spite of low ratings; but in Daytime, ratings and ratings alone determine whether a show will live or die.

Naturally, one can't help wondering how all this came about. In the war between art and commerce, how did commerce get such a firm grip on Daytime? Stay with me and we'll look into the question.

14

The Root of All Evil

Slightly the worse for wear, there's a small loose-leaf cookbook on my kitchen shelf that reads, "*Chatter with the Batter,* By Mother Barbour of Radio's *One Man's Family* . . . written by Minetta Ellen." The recipes, including a great one for lemon curd tart, are interspersed with Mother Barbour's "reminiscences" of her family and stills of the show's cast—in character, of course. The book was one of Standard Brands' give-aways of 1948. Since this particular copy was a gift from its author, I don't remember how many box tops or labels listeners had to send in to obtain one, or what the audience for it was at the time; but there, all these years later, my copy sits on its shelf, a mute witness to sponsors' early groping toward a science of market research.

From the mid-thirties, the efficacy of a radio soap opera was judged not only by how many people listened to it, but by how much of its sponsor's products it sold. This was measured in part by the audience response to give-aways—by how many coupons or box tops listeners mailed in to qualify for whatever enticing gift the announcer was touting. The technique often involved the show's writer, insofar as he frequently had to integrate the current gift into the show's dialogue. Mother Barbour, for instance, made frequent on-the-air comments about the cookbook as she was presumably putting it together.

There were also the Crossley and Hooper ratings, which I'll get to—but *sales* were what really mattered. When NBC's figures proved that purchases of Jergens Lotion rose in direct ratio to the number of times per month the buyers listened to the Walter Winchell show sponsored by Jergens, *that* was a meaningful statistic.

Oddly, this approach seems to have gone by the boards, in favor of the current industry-wide concern for demographics and a race for pure listenership, as evidenced by the Nielsen ratings.

But what, the reader may ask, has that to do with the subject matter of this book? Why is audience sampling of such earth-shaking importance to the writer of soap opera, anyway? To what extent does it affect what he writes? How did the whole system of network/affiliate/advertising-agent/sponsor/ratings come to be, anyway? It didn't just happen—it had to start somewhere. What were the forces that put soap opera—indeed all television—so firmly in the advertiser's control? And is it a good thing or a bad thing, or merely inevitable, like death and taxes?

It Pays to Advertise

It all started when a few industrial giants had the foresight to buy up the rights to Marconi's wireless almost as soon as it appeared on the scene, along with the rights to similar and sometimes infringing inventions. Even though the fledgling technology was years away from showing a profit, companies acquired patents, merged, or bought each other out—almost like an episode of *Dynasty*. And out in America's back yards, in garages and toolsheds, amateurs were experimenting with home-assembled sending or receiving sets until the airwaves were complete chaos, requiring the formation of a government agency (later the FCC) to impose a measure of order on the confusion.

At first everyone was more interested in the technology of radio than they were in what they were listening to, just so long as there was *something* coming in on that crystal set, or booming out of that loudspeaker. Early listeners were treated to phonograph records, prize fights, election returns, and musical renditions by self-styled "artists" who dropped in at the transmitting stations to offer their services free. Eventually someone at New York's station WEAF had a brainstorm and decided that individual messages could be broadcast at a slight charge; this came to be known as toll broadcasting and that was the earliest seed of today's fee-per-advertising-minute concept. By the end of 1922 a company could advertise its product by buying time on the air at the rate of $100 for ten minutes.

Compare that with the $32,000 per half-minute which advertisers are reputed to be paying this year on *All My Children*. On prime time the rate's even higher. Time marches on.

During the early 1920s, as transmission improved and as revenue from radio sales went into the tens of millions and doubled or tripled each year, the need for programming increased. But the volunteer artists the stations had been using until this time were proving unreliable in terms of showing up—or, of all things, they wanted to be paid! In addition, the composers of the songs that were sung or played (live or recorded) were reminding the stations somewhat testily that there was such a thing as copyright, and through ASCAP, were demanding fees. What to do?

Advertising, which was capable of meeting the looming rise in costs, was still officially frowned on, and acceptable only when it was couched in language so discreet as almost to defeat its purpose. Even so, the magazine *Radio Broadcast,* as quoted by historian Erik Barnouw, complained that "driblets of advertising, indirect but unmistakable, are floating through the ether every day . . . The woods are full of opportunists who are restrained by no scruples when the scent of profit comes down the wind." Businesses which did have the temerity to pay for programming shunned the term "sponsors," and instead were called "chaperones."

But by now the stakes were getting higher. A three-station link had been created via AT&T's long lines from New York's powerful station WEAF to a licensee station in Rhode Island to the home-owned station of a millionaire broadcaster in Massachusetts—the first network. By 1926 GE, RCA, and Westinghouse formed a new company, buying out WEAF and contracting for those long lines from AT&T. They called their new organization the National Broadcasting Company. Within the year another struggling young network had recapitalized with William S. Paley at its head, and became the Columbia Broadcasting System. (The American Broadcasting Company would not emerge until the early 1940s.) Broadcasting had become a huge business.

But how was it all to be paid for?

In this regard we should note that Britain in those early days began to levy an annual tax on each radio a householder owned; two decades later each television set would be similarly taxed. The money collected went to support the BBC, whose achievements in dramatic programming have been staggeringly impressive, up to and including the much loved *Upstairs, Downstairs.* The British chose one means of financing their broadcasting; we chose another—advertising.

Slowly, subtly, advertisers were getting the public used to direct sponsorship. Still restrained in their techniques, they were getting their listeners accustomed to associating certain artists or orchestras with certain products. The stations, instead of negotiating directly with sponsors, introduced another element into the picture; they paid a percentage of the total package to the ad agency representing the sponsor. "Thus," says historian

Barnouw, "advertising agencies were given a financial stake in a growing business and rising budgets." The agencies began to assume a larger role in radio production. By 1931, says Barnouw, "virtually all sponsored network programs were developed and produced by an advertising agency."

During World War II, in spite of severe shortages of consumer goods, radio advertising—and listenership—only *increased;* by the end of the war, two-thirds of all network programming was sponsored, in contrast to one-third before. By that time, however, a new factor was added to the equation. The first nonexperimental television shows had been broadcast in 1939.

The Essential Affiliates

But the network/affiliate/ad-agency/sponsor/ratings relationship had already taken shape during radio's heyday of the '20s and '30s, and the new technology would not change it appreciably except to increase revenues. What part did (and do) the affiliates play in all this?

Under FCC rules a network may "own and operate" only five VHF stations (channels 2 to 13 on the dial), and each must be located in a different area of the country. These are known as O and O's—Owned and Operated. Affiliates, on the other hand, are those stations contractually agreeing to carry a certain amount of a particular network's programming in exchange for a fee from the network. About 30 percent of the networks' income from time-sales goes to the affiliates. Each of the three major networks, by the way, has over two hundred affiliates.

This system guarantees the networks (and consequently the advertisers) a predictable number of viewers throughout the country. The affiliates, however, may elect to substitute local programming in place of some of the networks' offerings, and this affects the ratings of the shows not carried. Thus, when we hear that only 80 or 85 percent of a network's affiliates are carrying a particular Daytime drama, we know that show has an uphill task: winning back those affiliates so there are more viewers for the show and hence a wider market for the advertisers. Because television, both Daytime and prime time, is first and foremost an economic entity; television shows exist by the grace of their sponsors, and *the price the sponsors pay the networks per advertising half-minute depends on how many people can be counted on to watch the show.*

There's not an inflexible dollar-per-ratings-point figure; the price the sponsor or agency pays for time on a particular show is sometimes set months ahead. But a show's proven success, via the ratings, is a major consideration. And if, subsequently, the show doesn't do as well as anticipated, the network may try to compensate by giving the client extra advertising spots (called "make-goods").

At this point let's briefly consider the role of the agencies and their client-sponsors. There was a time when most television shows were produced by ad agencies. But how about the Daytime serial today? How much of the decision-making power, in terms of story and production, do the ad agencies exercise now?

Very little. In fact, there are only two agencies (Compton, with *Guiding Light, As the World Turns* and *Search for Tomorrow,* and Benton and Bowles with *Another World* and *Edge of Night*) that are still involved in Daytime in any production capacity—and their function is far more administrative than creative.

These five shows are owned and produced by Procter & Gamble, the sponsor, which has hired the agencies to help sell its soap (and toothpaste, mouthwash, and disposable diapers). P&G does exercise a good deal of creative control, though as I've mentioned it is relinquishing much of that control to the executive producers. But let's get back to the *agencies;* what precisely do they do?

When they *are* involved in production, agencies fill a number of functions. Compton, in its CBS shows, provides the facilities package (the below-the-line services and production facilities); they draw up the budget and see that it's adhered to; they handle contracts, payrolls, and benefits; they participate with the sponsor in negotiations with the network over the price of air time. They also figure in negotiations with the various talent unions when bargaining time rolls around. However, they no longer sit in on the story conferences.

How about the other shows? Who owns and/or produces them? And are they tied to any single agency?

No. *Days of Our Lives* is owned by executive Betty Corday and Columbia Pictures and is not answerable to any one agency, nor is *The Young and the Restless,* which is owned by John Conboy. As for ABC's "Love in the Afternoon" quintet, *Loving, Ryan's Hope, All My Children, One Life to Live,* and *General Hospital,*—all but *Loving* (owned by Agnes Nixon's corporation) are owned and produced by ABC, and no one ad agency is part of the configuration.

However, remember that it's the advertisers, individually or as represented by the large agencies, who provide the money which pays for scripts, actors, directors, producers, and network time. Without that constant infusion of advertiser money, soap opera would not exist. Nor would American television.

And the amount of money provided depends on the ratings.

By the Numbers

The earliest method of audience research developed was the Crossley system, inaugurated in 1930 and based on checkers phoning listeners to ask what shows they'd been tuned to in recent hours. Its sample audience was small, and its flaw was that the phone calls came after the fact and people's memories were not accurate. Also, many people in those days had radios but no telephones. Hooper ratings, developed five years later, reached a wider sampling and were more accurate, since the checking was done *during* the airing of a given program; but this system too depended on the telephone, still not universally owned. Both systems, however, did make an effort to determine the demographics of the listeners polled, by sex, race, age, and economic level. Even in those benighted days advertisers needed to know what kind of audience they were reaching, and whether the listeners could afford to buy the product advertised.

And then, in the mid-1940s came A.C. Nielsen.

The Nielsen ratings do not depend on telephone contact with the viewer. They depend on an Audimeter, a microcomputer attached (by agreement with the householder) to the tuner of the family's television sets as well as to its videotape recorder. The meter is connected with the Nielsen Company's central computer in Florida, and it can tell the parent computer what shows are turned on at any hour of the day or night. This information, data-processed, tells the ratings of any show for that week.

As of late 1983 there were 1,700 audimeters installed in homes nationwide, each of which is presumed to represent slightly fewer than 50,000 families. This figure is predicated on the theory that there are 83,800,000 television-viewing households across the country.

But that is only numbers. How about demographics? How do those little microcomputers know which member of the family, of what age or sex, is watching what show when? They don't. Consequently, the information received from Audimeters is augmented by information from diaries kept by another 2,400 families (more or less) and mailed in on a rotating basis every four weeks; the diaries keep track of the demographic information about each member of each viewing household.

How is all this supported? Advertisers and advertising agencies, networks and producers subscribe to the service, receiving the results on Thursday (for soap opera) of each week. A drop of a point or two in the ratings can produce panicked meetings of sponsors and producers on Friday.

What's the difference between ratings and shares? The rating of a show is based on the percentage of *all sets in the country* which are tuned

Peace between the generations? Don't you believe it. Daughter Laken (Julie Ronnie), mother Augusta (Louise Sorel) and grandmother-in-law Minx Lockridge (Dame Judith Anderson) in the newcomer Santa Barbara. *NBC photo.*

to that program. The share is *the share of all those sets that are turned on at that time.*

Ratings can run from about 9.5 points for the top-rated Daytime show down to about 3. (*The Doctors* was showing a rating of about 2.4 during the months before it was dropped; that's probably *why* it was dropped.) The share can go from 33 or thereabouts (*General Hospital, The Young and the Restless, All My Children*) or about a third of all sets turned on in that time slot, down to about 10. Because more people are at home at night than during the day, both ratings and shares tend to be a good deal higher during prime time. You'd think then that network prime time profits would be higher than Daytime profits, wouldn't you?

Wrong. Because production and time costs are lower in the daytime, profits can be higher than at night. It's long been an axiom that networks' profits from Daytime support lower profits or outright losses on prime time. For instance, in April of 1983 the Los Angeles *Times* stated that "ABC handily clears more than $1 million a week on *General Hospital's* average $2.7 million in ad revenues." This profit figure is generally conceded to be about twice that posed by nighttime's popular *Dallas.*

By way of further explanation, let's compare production costs. The same *Times* article says, "An established soap now cost $300,000 to $400,000 for a week's worth of hour-long episodes, or less than the cost of a single hour in prime time, where weekly costs for an hour-long series now range from $3.3 million to $5 million. "Now you know why soap operas are produced with such strict attention to economy. They have to support their free-spending nighttime relatives.

There's one other factor concerning ratings that we ought to take note of: the sweeps, which take place in November, February, and May. That's when the Nielsen company sends out 200,000 extra diaries—partly for the benefit of affiliate stations that can't afford to subscribe to the weekly ratings charts—and that's when the weekly ratings are scrutinized with extra care. Many important decisions are made then: the networks will base their new pricing structure on the sweeps figures, and the agencies will base their response on how much audience they're getting for their advertising dollar.

And how do the sweeps affect the writer? Most Daytime shows hype their storylines for those periods. For example, the headwriter, in conjunction with the producer, carefully plans a murder or court trial to take place then, which always boosts the ratings. All over the dial, major stories peak as an artificial stimulus to viewing. And the ratings will go up.

Counting Sand in the Sahara?

Opinions differ about the accuracy of the ratings system. Fred Allen is supposed to have said that audience ratings are like counting the grains of sand on the floor of a birdcage to find out how much sand is in the Sahara Desert. Art Buchwald says that if one Audimeter family went off to visit grandma, "that would mean 50,000 households had left the set to visit Grandma."

There are worrisome objections to the system. In a *TV Guide* interview in spring of 1983, Agnes Nixon said, "The ratings system we have is inadequate. We don't have measuring equipment in student-union lounges, or in office buildings where men and women watch. This mass of viewers has no opportunity to be counted."

She's right. All over the country there are people away from home who are watching Daytime—in hotels, in hospital wards, in the recreation rooms of mental hospitals and rest homes, in college dorms, and sorority and fraternity houses, in office buildings. There's an advertising agency in Los Angeles, for instance, where a dozen copywriters have all arranged a noon lunch hour so they can take their brown-bag lunches into one of the conference rooms and watch *All My Children.* For months the staff members of the Writers Guild of America West brought their lunch bags into the Guild board room to watch *The Doctors*—until it was canceled. Now they watch *Days of Our Lives* and *Another World.* These viewers and countless like them are not included among the metered households. How much difference does it make? Who can say?

Before we leave the subject, let's take a quick look at the kind of audience Daytime is reaching according to A.C. Nielsen's demographics, that is, the demographics of those viewers who are being measured. About 20,000,000 people watch one or more Soaps daily, about 50,000,000 weekly. Oddly, this is about the same number who watched in 1970, although there were only about three-fourths as many television sets then. In other words the percentage of people watching soap opera has actually declined in the last decade or so. We can only guess the reasons for these defections: competition from cable television, women entering the job market, or simply viewer disaffection. Also, the makeup of the Soap-watching audience has changed slightly. The percentage of men (now about 20 percent) and teenagers has risen, and certain shows (at least as of 1981) are attracting a much younger audience, *General Hospital* and *All My Children* in particular.

These two shows jockeyed for first place in the ratings race for several years, with *The Young and the Restless* now threatening them both. *General Hospital* actually hit its highest point with the Luke-Laura story in 1981;

two years later it had lost 27 percent of its viewers. Nevertheless, it leads the weekly charts more often then it lags (see Appendix). CBS has the pleasure, however, of knowing that the top-rated show during all the daylight hours is not a soap opera but the second half hour of one of its quiz shows, *The Price Is Right.* For soap opera programmers, this is bad news.

What is the profile of the average Daytime watcher? There isn't one, really, but *All My Children's* demographics probably appeal most to advertisers: as of 1981 it had the highest percentage of women viewers between 18 and 49 of all Daytime shows (67 percent). Some advertisers target an even younger group: women between 18 and 34. These groups are important because they spend more money on product.

But how about the earliest and staunchest soap opera viewers, the women over 50? Don't the advertisers care about them any more? The answer is nowhere stated, but it seems to be implicit in the changes that have been wrought in even such old-timers as *Guiding Light* and *As the World Turns.* Since 1981 these shows have changed utterly. The pace is faster, of course, but more important, both shows are now more jazzy and sexy; discos and cruise ships have replaced the kitchen kaffeeklatsch. The core families are being pushed into the background as attractive young newcomers take over the story lines.

The implications are interesting—and troublesome. Those faithful soap-watching women over fifty don't make as many household purchases as their younger counterparts. They're no longer raising children, so they're not buying as much toothpaste or laundry soap, or as many tennis shoes. With retirement (their own or their husband's) looming, their incomes will diminish. And (an even more depressing thought), they have fewer years of viewing ahead of them.

So although the reasons are economic rather than aesthetic, Daytime's targeting of the younger audience seems to reflect the attitude of society at large today: young is beautiful.

The Way the Money Goes

Since the major thrust of this chapter is really money, let's stay with it a bit longer and discuss what Daytime writers are paid. I've touched on a few aspects of this previously, but not in any detail; however, the associate writers' long journey from penury and obscurity might prove of interest.

Back in the early days of television soap opera, as I've said, most shows were produced under the aegis of the large ad agencies, or in some cases the large sponsors like P&G and Colgate-Palmolive. The Writers Guild, which for several decades has been bargaining out writers' salaries with film and television producers, had no contract with sponsors and agencies; hence it was open season on the employment of "dialoguers." The employers, who were in some cases the headwriters, could pay those poor benighted souls anything they wanted. And they did.

The result was sweatshop wages—at least compared to other writers in television.

After the Writers Guild strike of 1973 a settlement was reached with most of the ad agencies, the largest sponsors, the headwriters' corporations and the networks; for the first time associate writers could come out of their closets and stand upright. They were recognized, they were protected, and they were even guaranteed a modicum of credit—not much, but some.

If there wasn't dancing in the streets, there should have been. Two contracts later, after the strike of 1981, the current schedule of minimums was arrived at, with an upward adjustment each year until the contract terminates the end of February 1985. And by that time, one hopes, terms of a new three- or four-year contract will have been agreed upon.

What are the major provisions of the present schedule? I've already mentioned the minimums for a sample script. I've also mentioned that the least an associate may be paid per hour-script during the final year of the '81-'85 contract is $1,374. The minimum for a half-hour script is $743. (An experienced associate rarely settles for the minimum, however; he can usually bargain a much better deal for himself.) How about the headwriter's pay? He doesn't usually work for anything like the minimum; he can demand anything the traffic will bear, and sometimes those figures are very impressive indeed. But just for the record, let's see what's the very least he can receive.

There's something called a weekly aggregate minimum, which assumes that the headwriter will be employing all the associates himself and paying them out of what he's paid. That weekly figure, for an hour show, is $13,870. Sounds like a lot of money? Subtract from it the associates' minimum for five scripts (a total of $6,870), and the balance left over for the headwriter himself is $7,000. It still sounds princely, but out of that total he must pay his agent 10 percent; he must maintain a small army of secretaries, at least one bookkeeper, probably an attorney on retainer, and sometimes a medical adviser if the story line requires one. The telephone bill (to the producer in New York or Hollywood, or the sponsors in New Jersey or Cincinnati) can be catastrophic, and so can express-mail charges. Not to mention taxes. And if, as is now the custom, someone else does the break-downs and the editing, what happens? Further deductions—specifically, a little over $416 for each daily breakdown, or $2,080 for the week (for an hour show). That latter figure is the same for a writer hired to do the editing, if the headwriter doesn't do his own.

In other words, if all the headwriter has been able to ask for his serv-ices is scale, he should have stood in bed. However, he is usually a powerful person, much respected and much in demand, and he can pretty well ig-nore these minimums. Also, few headwriters are actually the employers of record anymore; P&G (through Compton) feels a show has more continuity if *they* employ the associate writers—so if a headwriter quits or is fired, he doesn't take the whole writing team with him. On shows like *General Hospi-tal* where the writing team is completely fractionated, each member of the team is employed by ABC; their salaries do not come out of the headwriter's pocket.

How about the long-term projection: is it paid for separately? No. The WGA contract assumes that writing the projection is included in the headwriter's normal duties and thus is not separately compensated. But how about the custom (vigorously frowned on by the WGA but pursued nonetheless by P&G and the networks) of hiring, behind the scenes and usually without the current headwriter's knowledge, another writer to write his own long-term projection as a sort of audition for the headwriter's job? What's the minimum he must receive for this clandestine task? The answer depends on the length of time the story lines will cover, ranging from $6,432 for a three-month projection to $12,864 for a year's worth of story. (In its '81 negotiations, the Writers Guild tried to outlaw this custom of having a poten-tial headwriter warming up in the wings, but that was one of the provisions that wasn't achieved.)

So when we read, as we did in a national news magazine a few years ago, that headwriter Pat Falken-Smith was being paid a half-million dollars a year for her headwriting services, we must remind ourselves that that glo-rious figure is gross, not net; and that by the time she finished paying her writing team and the rest of her professional entourage—and her taxes—there may not have been much money left over.

How about residuals, money paid for reruns? Residuals were agreed upon by the rest of the entertainment industry in 1960, and they are an im-portant part of the television writer's income; they tend to arrive when least expected and are what keeps a writer afloat between jobs. However, there are no domestic reruns for soap opera. A few Daytime shows (*General Hos-pital, Another World, Search for Tomorrow,* and *Days of Our Lives*) are

Happily ever after? Michael Tylo and Lisa Brown as Quint and Nola on CBS's Guiding Light*. CBS photo.*

syndicated abroad, and the Guild contract provides the writing team with a percentage figure for such showings—but for writers not on those four shows the subject is academic so we won't go into the figures here.

Of major importance to every Daytime writer, however, are his fringe benefits. His employer (headwriter, network, sponsor, or owner) must pay 6 percent of the writer's salary into the Writers Guild-Industry Pension Plan, and 4 percent into the Health Plan. These sums (also paid on the headwriter's salary) are not deducted from the writer's salary, but are paid in addition to it. So if this author indicates a bias in favor of the Writers Guild, it is because the Guild has provided her with health insurance, dental coverage, extra income for her later years—and has done much to correct the exploitative salaries of a decade and a half ago. In Union There Is Strength.

One area, however, still needs attention: individual credit for the Daytime writer. In this regard the ABC shows are far better than their competitors, where only joint credit is given and then as infrequently as the Guild contract allows. In most cases, writing credits are run on the crawl only about twice a week, and the whole writing team is listed; there's no way of knowing who wrote what show. There are times—not as often as one would like perhaps—when one has poured one's heart into a show, felt like Chekhov during the writing of it, and longed to see one's name, along with the headwriter's of course, attached to it. But no. If it's a day when the credits are listed at all, the whole team gets credit. It's enough to make a stone weep.

This brings us back to the opening subject of this chapter: the power of the advertiser in soap opera. If one network can give the individual associate credit for his work, why can't the others?

I know the arguments; I heard them during contract negotiations—the cost. It costs money to mount individual credit titles which differ from day to day. And it takes time to run the credit crawl not just twice but five times a week, subtracting from the time available for sale to the advertisers. Every half-minute counts. Every *second* counts. So up to the present time, most Daytime employers have held fast against granting daily, individual credits.

But maybe some day . . . who knows?

Well, there they are: the terms of our indenture. Are they worth the effort? I think so.

Granted, the market for our services is small. A couple of daytime dramas have been launched on Cable, taking advantage of their non-network status to handle sexier material than commercial stations allow;

but these efforts thus far have been short-lived. There is one religious soap opera broadcasting on cable out of the South, with considerable success. And there are what I've referred to as the neo-soaps—nighttime once-a-week dramatic series like *Dynasty* and *Dallas* (of which when asked by a participant at that soap opera convention whether he thought they were "competition," Henry Slesar said, "No, they're exoneration"). However, these nighttime cousins of traditional Soaps tend to be more hard-hitting than Daytime shows, are vastly more expensive to produce, and for whatever reason, are usually written not by experienced Soap writers but by established primetime writers. They reach, after all, a different audience, and the rules of the game are different.

In any event, here we are, a little band of brothers (and sisters) laboring in the vineyards of our chosen medium. And I can tell you honestly that we love the job—love it in spite of the frantic pace, the last-minute emergencies, the wall-to-wall work, and the frustration of knowing that we contribute only a portion of the finished product. Because though we must (and do) accept the fact that Daytime's primary task is to increase its audience and sell its product, we know there is still room within the form for every observation we want to make about the human condition.

15
L'Envoi

In one of Southern California's fashionable new malls, there is a Mexican restaurant on the upper level, with a terrace looking out over a few intervening rooftops to the ocean beyond. Smells drift out temptingly from the café's kitchen: tamales and frijoles, tortillas and chiles rellenos. And beside the entrance, posted on a window, is an announcement designed to lure the busy shopper inside—not the day's luncheon special as you might expect, but something even more enticing. It reads:

THE YOUNG AND THE RESTLESS	11-12
ALL MY CHILDREN	12-1
ONE LIFE TO LIVE	1-2
GENERAL HOSPITAL	2-3

To those viewers, and their countless fellows across the country—and to every writer and would-be writer who may one day wish to try his hand at writing Daytime drama—this book is affectionately addressed.

Appendix

Writers Guild of America Awards

Daytime Serial Writing: Winners

1/1/72 thru 12/31/73—presented 1973:
Loring Mandel, Nancy Ford, Louis Ringwald, Mac McClellan
"LOVE OF LIFE"

1/1/73 thru 12/31/73—presented 1974:
Ralph Ellis & Eugenie Hunt with Bibi Wein & Jane Chambers
"SEARCH FOR TOMORROW"

1/1/74 thru 12/31/74—presented 1975:
Ann Marcus, Joyce Perry, Pamela Wylie, Ray Goldstone
"SEARCH FOR TOMORROW"

1/1/75 thru 12/31/75—presented 1976:
Claire Labine, Paul Mayer, Mary Munisteri, Allan Leicht
"RYAN'S HOPE"

1/1/76 thru 12/31/76—presented 1977:
Claire Labine, Paul Avila Mayer, Mary Munisteri, Jeffrey Lane
"RYAN'S HOPE"

1/1/77 thru 12/31/77—presented 1978:
Claire Labine, Paul Avila Mayer, Mary Munisteri
"RYAN'S HOPE"

1/1/78 thru 12/31/78—presented 1979:
Claire Labine, Jeffrey Lane, Paul Avila Mayer, Mary Munisteri, Judith Pinsker
"ONE LIFE TO LIVE"

1/1/79 thru 12/31/79—presented 1980:
Jerome and Bridget Dobson, Chuck and Patti Dizenzo, Robert and Phyllis White, Robert Soderberg, Jean Rouverol
"GUIDING LIGHT"

1/1/80 thru 8/31/80—presented 1981:
Claire Labine, Paul Avila Mayer, Mary Munisteri, Jeffrey Lane
"RYAN'S HOPE"

9/1/80 thru 8/31/81—presented 1982:
Claire Labine, Paul Avila Mayer, Mary Ryan Munisteri, Jeffrey Lane
"RYAN'S HOPE"

9/1/81 thru 8/31/82—presented 1983:
Claire Labine, Mary Ryan Munisteri, Eugene Price, Barbara Perlman, Rory Metcalf
"RYAN'S HOPE"

9/1/82 thru 8/31/83—presented 1984:
Claire Labine, Paul Avila Mayer, Mary Ryan Munisteri, Nancy Ford
"RYAN'S HOPE"

Emmy Awards for Daytime Writing

The National Academy of Television Arts and Sciences' "Emmy" Awards for Outstanding Writing for a Daytime Drama Series:

'73-'74: Henry Slesar
EDGE OF NIGHT (CBS)

'74-'75: Harding Lemay, Tom King, Charles Kozloff, Jan Merlin, Douglas Marland
ANOTHER WORLD (NBC)

'75-'76: Will J. Bell, Kay Lenard, Pat Falken Smith, Bill Rega, Margaret Sherwood, Sheri Anderson, Wanda Coleman
DAYS OF OUR LIVES (CBS)

'76-'77: Claire Labine, Paul Avila Mayer, Mary Munisteri
RYAN'S HOPE (ABC)

'77-'78: Claire Labine, Paul Avila Mayer, Mary Munisteri, Allen Leicht, Judith Pinsker
RYAN'S HOPE (ABC)

'78-'79: Claire Labine, Paul Avila Mayer, Mary Munisteri, Judith Pinsker, Jeffrey Lane
RYAN'S HOPE (ABC)

'79-'80: Claire Labine, Paul Avila Mayer, Mary Munisteri, Judith Pinsker
RYAN'S HOPE (ABC)

'80-'81: Douglas Marland, Robert Dwyer, Nancy Franklin, Harding Lemay
GUIDING LIGHT(CBS)

'81-'82: Douglas Marland, Nancy Franklin, Patrick Mulcahy, Gene Palumbo, Frank Salisbury
THE GUIDING LIGHT (CBS)

'82-'83: Claire Labine, Paul Avila Mayer, Mary Ryan Munisteri, Eugene Price, Judith Pinsker, Nancy Ford, B.K. Perlman, Rory Metcalf, Trent Jones
RYAN'S HOPE (ABC)

Note: Although the Academy first began to give awards in 1948, Daytime Emmy's were not included until the '73-'74 season. All awards for Daytime Programming are now presented at a separate ceremony in New York in late Spring or early Summer.

Ratings and Shares

Here are the ratings of Daytime Dramas, as compiled by A.C. Nielsen Co. for the week of Feb. 26, 1984:

SHOW:	NETWORK	RATING	SHARE
GENERAL HOSPITAL	ABC	10	30
YOUNG AND THE RESTLESS	CBS	9.7	33
ALL MY CHILDREN	ABC	9.2	28
GUIDING LIGHT	CBS	9.0	27
AS THE WORLD TURNS	CBS	8.6	27
ONE LIFE TO LIVE	ABC	8.0	26
DAYS OF OUR LIVES	NBC	7.5	23
CAPITOL	CBS	6.8	23
ANOTHER WORLD	NBC	5.5	18
RYAN'S HOPE	ABC	5.1	17
LOVING	ABC	4.2	16
SEARCH FOR TOMORROW	NBC	3.4	12
EDGE OF NIGHT	ABC	3.3	10

Reference Sources

The numbers listed below are reprinted with permission from the *NEWSLETTER* of Writers Guild of America, West. Unless otherwise indicated, all numbers are in the 213 area code:

Air Force 209-7511
Air Pollution 484-9300
Alcoholism Info 821-3228
Am. Humane Assn. 653-3394
Amnesty Int'l. 388-1237
Animals 841-5300
Army 209-7621
Arthritis 938-6111
Aviation/Aerospace 390-3339

Blind 663-1111
Board of Education 625-6766
   (Work Permits, etc) 687-4831
Boy Scouts 413-4400

Catholics Ext. 214, 388-8101
Chicanos 224-2544
Coast Guard 548-2302
CPR 823-8400
Credit Union 939-4228
Customs Service 688-5939

Drugs, Federal Agcy. 688-4343

Epilepsy 382-7337

Fair Housing Council 781-6940
Family Counseling Ext. 11, 465-5131
F.B.I. 272-6161
Food & Drug Adm. 688-3771
Food/Hunger 449-2714
Forestry Industry 462-7278

Gays 851-4997

Handicapped 461-8358
Ham Radio 872-1089
Health Fund 659-7100
Hypnotists 988-5550

Immigration/Naturalization 688-2119
Italians 467-3656

Jews Ext. 407, 852-1234

Kidney Disease 641-8152

Labor Dept. 688-4970
Law (ABA) (312) 621-9200

Marine Corps. 209-7272
Medical (AMA) (800) 621-4115
M.P. Health & Welfare 877-0991/985-9022
M.P. & TV Fund 937-7250

Navy 209-7481
Nurses, Critical Care (714) 752-8191

Organ Gift/Transplant 641-5245

Pedophilia 478-3852
Pension Plan 659-6430
Plastic Surgeons (800) 722-2777
Police Dept. 485-3586
Population/Birth Control 273-2101
Probate/Parole 896-8545/989-8878
Probation Ext. 2851, 923-7721
Psychiatric Society 477-1041

Red Cross 384-5261

Safety Council 385-6461
Sheriff 974-4228
Social Workers 935-2050
State Filming Info. 736-2465

Telephone Matters 986-1460

Underwater 908-9541

Vaudeville/Theater History 623-9100
Vietnam Veterans (714) 235-9731
Veterinarians 723-1746

War and Peace 457-1131
Women's Issues 974-7601

YMCA (Nat'l) 783-5436

The numbers listed below are reprinted, with permission, from the *NEWSLETTER* of Writers Guild of America, East. Unless otherwise indicated, all numbers are in the 212 area code:

Alcoholism Information and Referral Service 935-7070
American Bar Association (312) 621-1703
American Medical Association Hotline (800) 621-4115
Archdiocese of New York 371-1000

Better Business Bureau 533-6200
Boy Scouts of America 242-1100
Board of Elections (NYC) 924-1860

Coast Guard 688-7000
Courts (New York State, Information) 587-4000

Environmental Protection Agency 264-2657

Fire Department (NYC, Information) 403-1544
F.B.I. 553-2700

Health Department (NYC) 285-9503

Jewish Theological Seminary 678-8018

Lexington School for the Deaf 899-8800
Lighthouse (Association for the Blind) 355-2200

New York Society Library (NYC History) 288-6900
New York State Historical Society 873-3400

Police Department (NYC, Information) 374-5000

U.S. Armed Services (Office of Public Affairs) 688-7572
UNESCO, UNICEF and World Health Organizations (United Nations) 754-1234
U.S. Information Agency (Education and Cultural Affairs) 620-6752
U.S. Information Agency (Motion Picture and TV Service) 399-5664
U.S. Navy 834-2793

Literary Agencies

We suggest that the individual first write or telephone the agency, detail his professional and/or academic credentials and briefly describe the nature of the material he desires to submit. The agency will then advise the individual whether it is interested in receiving the material with a view toward representing it.

Most agencies, as a courtesy to writers, will return material sent to them if a self-addressed stamped envelope accompanies the submission. However, should a submission not be returned for any reason, the individual should be aware that the agency is under no obligation to return literary material to a writer seeking representation. The Guild cannot assist in seeking the return of material.

We regret we can offer no assistance in finding, selecting, or recommending an agent.

(*) This agency has indicated that it will consider unsolicited material from writers.

(**) This agency has indicated that it will consider unsolicited material from writers only as a result of references from persons known to it.

(P) Indicates packaging agency.

(S) Society of Authors Representatives—signed thru WGAE only.

The following agencies have subscribed to the Writers Guild of America-Artists' Manager Basic Agreement to 1976:

*Act 48 Mgmt., 1501 Broadway, #1713, NY (10036), 212/354-4250

Adams Limited, Bret, 448 W. 44th St., NY (10036), 212/765-5630

**Adams, Ray & Rosenberg, (P), 9200 Sunset Blvd. PH 25, LA (90069), 278-3000

**Agency For The Performing Arts, (P), 9000 Sunset Bl., #1200, LA (90069), 273-0744

Agency For The Performing Arts, (P), 888 7th Ave., NY (10016), 212/582-1500

*All Talent Agency, 2437 E. Washington Bl., Pasadena (91104), 797-2422

*Allan Agency, Lee, 4571 N. 68th St., Milwaukee, WI (53218), 414/463-7441

**Altoni, Buddy, PO Box 1022, Newport Beach, CA (92663), 714/851-1711

Amsel & Assoc., Fred, 291 S. La Cienega Blvd., #307, BH (90211), 855-1200

**Animal Crackers Entertainment, 215 Riverside Dr., Newport Beach (92663), 714/645-4726 or 435-0255

Artists Agency, The (P), 10000 Santa Monica Bl., #305, LA (90067), 277-7779

**Artists Career Mgmt., 8295 Sunset Blvd., LA (90046), 654-6650

Artists' Entertainment Agency (P), 10100 Santa Monica Blvd., #348, LA (90067), 557-2507

*Artists Group, The, 10100 Santa Monica Bl., #310, LA (90067), 552-1100

Associated Artists Mgmt., 1501 Broadway, #1808A, NY (10036), 212/398-0460

**Associated Talent Agency, 8816 Burton Way, BH (90211), 271-4662

Ballard Talent Agency, Mark, 1915 W. Glenoaks Blvd., #200, Glendale (91201), 841-8305

*Barnett Agency, Gary Jay, Box 333 Bay Station, Brooklyn, NY (11235), 212/332-2894

Barskin Agency, The, 11240 Magnolia Bl., #201, NH (91601), 985-2992

**Bauman & Hiller 271-5601

Beakel & Jennings Agency, 427 N. Canon Dr., #205, BH (90210), 274-5418

Berger Associates, Bill (S), 444 E. 58th St., NY (10022), 212/486-9588

**Berkeley Square Literary Agency, P.O. Box 25324, LA (90025), 207-3704

Berman, Lois, 430 W. 44th St., NY (10036)

**Bernacchi & Assoc., Shauna, 1100 Glendon Ave., LA (90024), 824-0542

Bernstein, Ron, 119 W. 57th St., NY (10019), 212/265-0750

Big Red Talent Ent., 8330 Third St., LA (90048), 463-4982

Blassingame, McCauley & Wood (S), 60 E. 42nd St., NY (10017)

**Bloom, Levy, Shorr & Assoc., 800 S. Robertson Blvd., LA (90035), 659-6160

Bloom, Harry, 8833 Sunset Blvd., #202, LA (90069), 659-5985

Bloom, J. Michael, 400 Madison Ave., 20th Fl., NY (10017), 212/832-6900

Bloom, J. Michael, 9200 Sunset Bl., #1210, LA (90069), 275-6800

Blue Star Agency, P.O. Box 2754, Arlington, VA (22202)

Brandon & Assoc., Paul, 9046 Sunset Bl., LA (90069), 273-6173

Brandt & Brandt (S), 1501 Broadway, NY (10036), 212/840-5760

Breltner Literary Assoc., Susan, 1650 Broadway #501, NY (10019)

Brebner Agencies, 185 Berry St., Bldg. 2, #144, SF (94017), 415/495-6700

Brewis Agency, Alex, 8721 Sunset Bl., LA (90069), 274-9874

**Broder/Kurland Agency, The (P), 9046 Sunset Bl., #202, LA (90069), 274-8921

*Brody, Howard T., P.O. Box 291423, Davis, FL (33329), 305/587-2863

Brooke-Dunn-Oliver, 9165 Sunset Blvd., #202, LA (90069), 859-1405

Brown Agency, J., 8733 Sunset Blvd., #102, LA (90069), 550-0296

Brown, Ltd., Curtis (S), 575 Madison Ave., NY (10022), 212/755-4200

Brown, Ned, 407 N. Maple Dr., BH (90210), 276-1131

*BTV Ltd., P.O. Box 460, NY (10016), 212/696-5419

Buchwald & Assoc., Don, 10 E. 44th St., NY (10017), 212/867-1070

*Butler, Ruth, 8622 Reseda Bl., #211, Northridge (91324), 886-8440

Calder Agency, 4150 Riverside Dr., Burbank (91505), 845-7434

Career Mgmt., 435 S. La Cienega Blvd., #108, LA (90048), 657-1020

*Carpenter Co., 1434 6th Ave., San Diego (92101), 619/235-8482

Carroll Agency, William, 448 N. Golden Mall, Burbank (91502), 848-9948

Carvanis Agency, Maria, 235 West End Ave., NY (10023), 212/580-1559

**Case, Bertha, 345 W. 58th St., NY (10019), 212/541-9451

Catalytic Agent, The, 685 West End Ave., NY (10025), 212/666-3991

**Cavaleri & Associates, 6605 Hollywood Blvd., #220, Hwd. (90028), 461-2940

Charter Mgmt., 9000 Sunset Blvd., #1112, LA (90069), 278-1690

Chasin-Park-Citron Agency, 9255 Sunset Bl., LA (90069), 273-7190

Chasman & Strick, Assoc., 6725 Sunset Bl., #506, Hwd (90028), 463-1115

Clients' Agency, The, 2029 Century Park East, #1330, LA (90067), 277-8492

CNA & Associates, 8721 Sunset Blvd., #102, LA (90069), 657-2063

Colton, Kingsley & Assoc., 321 S. Beverly Dr., BH (90212), 277-5491

Connell & Assoc., Polly, 4605 Lankershim Bl., NH (91602), 985-6266

Contemporary-Korman Artists, 132 Lasky Dr., BH (90212) 278-8250

**Conway & Assoc., Ben, 999 N. Doheny Dr., LA (90069), 271-8133

Cooper Agency, The (P), 1900 Ave. of the Stars, #2535, LA (90067), 277-8422

Creative Artists Agency (P), 1888 Century Pk. E., LA (90067), 277-4545

*Cumber Attractions, Ltd. 6615 Sunset Blvd., Hwd. (90028), 469-1919

C.W.A. Chateau of Talent, 1633 Vista Del Mar, Hwd. (90018), 461-2727

**D, H, K, P, R, 7319 Beverly Bl., LA (90036) 857-1234

*D.J. Enterprises, 339 S. Franklin St., Allentown, PA (18102), 215/437-0723

DMI Talent Agency, 250 W. 57th St., #713, NY (10107), 212/246-4650

Dade/Rosen Assoc., 9172 Sunset Bl., #2, LA (90069), 278-7077

*Dalmler Artists Agency, 2007 Wilshire Blvd, #808, LA (90057), 483-9783

**Davis Agency, Dona Lee, 3518 W. Cahuenga Blvd., Hwd (90068), 850-1205

**Dellwood Enterprises, 409 N. Camden Dr., #206, BH (90210), 271-7847

DeMille Talent Agency, Diana, 12457 Ventura Blvd., #104, SC (91604), 761-7171

Dennis, Karg, Dennis and Co., 470 S. San Vicente Blvd., LA (90048), 651-1700

Diamant, Anita (S), 51 E. 42nd St., NY (10017)

**Diamond Artists, 9200 Sunset Blvd.,, #909, LA (90069), 278-8146

Donadio & Associates, Candida (S), 111 W. 57th St., NY (10019), 212/757-7076

**Dorese Agency, Alyss Barlow, 41 W. 82nd St., NY (10024), 212/580-2855

**Dubose Associates, Albert, One Sherman Square, NY (10023), 212/580-9790

Elsenbach-Greene (P), 760 N. La Cienega Bl., LA (90069), 659-3420

Elmo Agency, Ann (S), 60 E. 42nd St., NY (10165), 212/661-2880

Exclusive Artists Agency, 4040 Vineland Blvd., #225, SC (91604), 761-1154

Ferguson & Berry Talent Agency, 1090 S. La Brea Ave., #201, LA (90019), 857-0519

Ferrell Agency, Carol, 708-7773

Film Artists Mgmt. Enterprises, 8278 Sunset Blvd., LA (90046), 556-8071

Fischer Co. Sy, (P), 1 E. 57th St., NY (10022), 212/486-0426

Fischer Co., Sy (P), 10960 Wilshire Blvd., #922, LA (90024), 557-0388

Fox Chase Agency (S), 419 E. 57th St., NY (10022), 212/752-8211

Freeman-Wyckoff & Assoc., 6331 Hollywood Bl., #1122, LA (90028), 464-4866

Frings Agency, Kurt, 415 S. Crescent Dr., #320, BH (90210), 274-8881

*Garrick Int'l Agency, Dale, 8831 Sunset Blvd., LA (90069), 657-2661

Geddes Agency, 8749 Holloway Dr., LA (90069), 657-3392

**Gerard, Paul, 2918 Alta Vista, Newport Beach, CA (92660), 714-7950

Gerritsen International, 8721 Sunset Blvd.,#203, LA (90069), 659-8414

Gersh Agency Inc., The, 222 N. Canon Dr., BH (90210), 274-6611

Gibson Agency, J. Carter, 9000 Sunset Blvd., #811, LA (90069), 274-8813

**GMA, 1741 N. Ivar St., #221, Hwd. (90028), 466-7161

Gold Talent Agency, Harry, 8295 Sunset Blvd., #202, LA (90064), 654-5550

Goldman & Novell Agency, The, 6383 Wilshire Blvd., #115, LA (90048), 651-4578

Goldstein & Assoc., Allen, 9000 Sunset Blvd., #1105, LA (90069), 278-5005

Grashin Agency, Mauri, 8170 Beverly Bl., #109, LA (90048), 651-1828

Green Agency, Ivan, The, 1888 Century Pk., #908, LA (90067), 277-1541

Groffsky Literary Agency, Maxine, 2 Fifth Ave., NY (10011), 212/677-2720

Grossman & Assoc., Larry, 211 S. Beverly Dr., #206, BH (90212), 550-8127

Grossman-Staimaster Agency, 10100 Santa Monica Blvd., #310, LA (90067), 552-0905

**Halsey Agency, Reece, 8733 Sunset Bl., LA (90069), 652-2409
Hamilburg Agency, Mitchell, 292 S. La Cienega Bl., BH (90211), 657-1501
**Hannaway-We-Go, 1741 N. Ivar St., #102, Hwd (90028), 854-3999
**Harris Mgmt., Mark, 10100 Santa Monica Blvd., #310, LA (90067), 552-1100
Harvey, Helen (S), 410 W. 24th St., NY (10011), 212/675-4445
**Heacock Literary Agency, Inc., 1523 6th St., SM (90401), 393-6227
**Henderson/Hogan Agency, 247 S. Beverly Dr., BH (90212), 274-7815
Henderson/Hogan Agency, 200 W. 57th St., NY (10019), 212/765-5190
**Henry, Kevin Jon, 2301 Westwood Blvd., LA (90064), 475-9737
**Hesseltine/Baker Associates, 165 W. 46th St., #409, NY (10036), 212/921-4460 LETTERS ONLY
Holland Agency, Calvin Bruce, 1836 E. 18th St., Brooklyn, NY (11229), 212/375-4863
*Hollywood Talent Agency, 213 Brock Ave., Toronto, Ont., Canada M6K 2L8, 416/531-3180
*Hostetter, Esq., J. Ross, 8300 Douglas Ave., #800, Dallas, TX (75225), 214/363-6684
Hudson, Scott C., 215 E. 76th St., NY (10021), 212/570-9645
**Hunt Mgmt, Diana, 44 W. 44th St., #1414, NY (10036), 212/391-4971
**Hunt & Associates, George, 8350 Santa Monica Bl., LA (90069), 654-6600
**Hussong Agency, Robert, 721 N. La Brea Ave., #201, Hwd. (90038), 655-2534
*Hyman, Ansley Q., 3123 Cahuenga Bl. W., LA (90068), 851-9198

**Imison Playwrights Ltd., Michael, 150 W. 47th St., #SF, NY (10036), 212/921-2123
International Creative Mgmt., (P), 8899 Beverly Blvd., LA (90048), 550-4000
International Creative Mgmt., (P), 40 W. 57th St., NY (10019), 212/556-5600
International Literary Agents, 9000 Sunset Blvd., #1115, LA (90069), 874-2563

*Jaffe Representatives, 140 7th Ave., #2L, NY (10011), 212/741-1359
*Joseph/Knight Agency, 6331 Hollywood Blvd., #924, Hwd. (90028), 465-5474

*Kalmus, Michael L., 90 Gold St., NY (10038), 212/732-0127

Kane Agency, Merrily, 9171 Wilshire Blvd., #310, BH (90210), 550-8874
**Kaplan-Stahler Agency, 119 N. San Vicente Blvd., BH (90211), 653-4483
Karlan Agency, Patricia, 12345 Ventura Blvd., #T, SC (91604), 506-5666
**Karlin Agency, Larry, 10850 Wilshire Blvd., #600, LA (90024), 475-4828
*Kerwin Agency, Wm., 1605 N. Cahuenga Blvd., #202, Hwd. (90028), 469-5155
**Keynan-Goff Assoc., 2049 Century Park East, #4370, LA (90067), 556-0339
*Kimberly Agency, 3950 W. 6th St., #203, LA (90020), 738-6087
*King, Ltd., Archer, 1440 Broadway, #2100, NY (10018), 212/764-3505
*King Agency, Howard, 9060 Santa Monica Blvd., #104, LA (90069), 858-8048
*Kingsley Corp, 112 Barnsbee Ln., Coventry, CT (06238), 203/742-9575
**Kohner Agency, Paul, (P), 9169 Sunset Blvd., LA (90069), 550-1060
**Kopaloff Company, The, 9046 Sunset Blvd., , #201, LA (90069), 273-6173
*Kratz & Co., 210 5th Ave., NY (10010), 212/683-9222
Kroll Agency, Lucy, (S), 390 West End Ave., NY (10024), 212/877-0627

**Lake Office, Candace, 1103 Glendon Ave., LA (90024), 824-9706
Lantz Office, The, 888 Seventh Ave., NY (10106), 212/586-0200
Lantz Office, The, 9255 Sunset Blvd., #505, LA (90069), 858-1144
Lazar, Irving Paul, 211 S. Beverly Dr., BH (90212), 275-6153
**Leading Artists, Inc., (P), 1900 Ave. of the Stars, #1530, LA (90067), 277-9090
*Lee Literary Agency, L. Harry, Box 203, Rocky Point, NY (11778), 516/744-1188, LETTERS ONLY
Lenny Assoc., Jack, 9701 Wilshire Blvd., BH (90212), 271-2174
Lenny Assoc., Jack, 140 W. 58th St., NY (10019), 212/582-0272
Light Co., The, 113 N. Robertson Blvd., LA (90048), 273-9602
Light Co., The, 1443 Wazee St., 3rd Fl., Denver, CO (80202), 303/572-8363
**Literary Artists Mgmt., P.O. Box 1604, Monterey, CA (93940), 408/899-7145
Literary Associates, 9701 Wilshire Blvd., #850, BH (90212), 550-0077
Literistic, Ltd., 32 W. 40th St., NY (10018), 212/944-1160
*London Star Promotions, 7131 Owensmouth Ave., #C116, Canoga Park (91303), 709-0447
Loo, Bessie, 8235 Santa Monica Blvd., LA (90046), 650-1300
Lund Agency, The, 6515 Sunset Blvd., #304, Hwd. (90028), 466-8280
Lynne & Reilly Agency, 6290 Sunset Blvd., #1002, Hwd. (90028), 461-2828
Lyons Agency, Grace, 204 S. Beverly Dr., #102, BH (90212), 652-5290

Major Talent Agency, (P), 1182 San Vicente Blvd., #510, LA (90049), 820-5841

*Maris Agency, 17620 Sherman Way, #8, Van Nuys, CA (91406), 708-2493

Markson Lit. Agency, Elaine, 44 Greenwich Ave., NY (10011), 212/243-8480

**Markson Literary Agency, Raya, 6015 Santa Monica Blvd., Hwd. (90038), 552-2083

**Matson Co., Harold, 276 5th Ave., NY (10001), 212/679-4490

McCartt, Oreck, Barrett, 9200 Sunset Blvd., #531, Hwd. (90069), 278-6243

McIntosh & Otis (S), 475 5th Ave., NY (10017), 212/689-1050

Medford Agency, Ben, 139 S. Beverly Dr., #329, BH (90212), 278-0017

Merit Agency, The, 12926 Riverside Dr., #C, SO (91423), 986-3017

Merrill, Helen (S), 337 W. 22nd St., NY (10011), 212/924-6314

Messenger Agency, Fred, 8235 Santa Monica Blvd., LA (90046), 654-3800

**Miller Agency, Peter, The., P.O. Box 764, Midtown Station, NY (10018), 212/221-8329

**Mills, Ltd., Robert P., 333 5th Ave., NY (10016), 212/685-6575

Morris Agency, William (P), 151 El Camino Dr., BH (90212), 274-7451

Morris Agency, William (P), 1350 Ave. of the Americas, NY (10019), 212/586-5100

Morton Agency, 1105 Glendon Ave., LA (90024), 824-4089

**Moss, Marvin, (P), 9200 Sunset Blvd., LA (90069), 274-8483

**Nachtigall Agency, The, 1885 Lombard St., SF (94123), 415/346-1115

Neighbors, Charles, 240 Waverly Pl., NY (10014), 212/924-8296

Ober & Associates, Harold (S), 40 E. 49th St., NY (10017), 212/759-8600

Oscard Assoc., Fifi, 19 W. 44th St., NY (10022), 212/764-1100

*Panda Agency, 3721 Hoen Ave. Santa Rosa, CA (95405), 707/544-3671

Paramuse Artists Associates, 1414 Avenue of the Americas, NY (10019), 212/758-5055

Phoenix Literary Agency, 150 E. 74th St., NY (10021), 212/838-4060

**Pleshette Agency, Lynn, 2700 N. Beachwood Dr., Hwd. (90068), 465-0428

**Preminger Agency, Jim, (P), 1650 Westwood Blvd., #201, LA (90024), 475-9491

Prescott Agency, Guy, The, 8920 Wonderland Ave., LA (90046), 656-1963

*Professional Authors Literary Services, 4237-2 Keanu St., Honolulu HI (96816), 808/734-5469

Progressive Artists Agency, 400 S. Beverly Dr., BH (90212), 553-8561

*Protter, Susan Ann, 110 W. 40th St., #1408, NY (10018), 212/840-0480

Raines & Raines (S), 475 5th Ave., NY (10017), 212/684-5160

Raper Enterprises Agency, 9441 Wilshire Blvd. #620D, BH (90210), 273-7704

Rappa Agency, Ray, 7471 Melrose Ave., #11, LA (90046), 650-1190

**Regency Artists Ltd., 9200 Sunset Blvd., #823, LA (90069), 273-7103

*Rhodes Literary Agency, 140 West End Ave., NY (10023), 212/580-1300 LETTERS ONLY

**Richland Agency, The, 1888 Century Park East, #1107, LA (90067), 553-1257

Roberts Co., The, 427 N. Canon Dr., BH (90210), 275-9384

*Roberts, Flora, 157 W. 57th St., NY (10019), 212/355-4165

Robinson-Luttrell & Assoc., 141 El Camino Dr., #110, BH (90212), 275-6114

**Rogers & Assoc., Stephanie, 9100 Sunset Blvd., #340, LA (90069), 278-2015

Rose Agency, Jack, 6430 Sunset Blvd., #1203, Hwd. (90028), 463-7300

**Rosenstone/Wender, 3 E. 48th St., NY (10017), 212/832-8330

**Ross Assoc., Eric, 60 E. 42nd St, #426, NY (10017), 212/687-9797

Russell & Volkening, Inc., 551 5th Ave., NY (10017), 212/682-5340

Sackheim Agency, The, 9301 Wilshire Blvd., , BH (90210), 858-0606

Safler, Gloria, (S), 667 Madison Ave., NY (10021), 212/838-4868

**Sanders' Agency, Honey, 229 W. 42nd St., #404, NY (10036), 212/947-5555

**Sanders Agency, Norah, 1100 Glendon Ave, PH, LA (90024), 824-2264

**San Fran. Agency, 899 E. Francisco Blvd. E, San Rafael (94901), 415/456-7140

**Sanford-Beckett Agency, 1015 Gayley Ave., LA (90024), 208-2100

*SBK Assoc., 11 Chamberlain, Waltham, MA (02154), 617/894-4037

**Schecter, Irv, (P), 9300 Wilshire Blvd., #410, BH (90212), 278-8070

*Schuster-Dowdell Org., The, P.O. Box 2, Valhalla, NY (10595), 914/761-3106

*Selected Artists Agency, 12711 Ventura Blvd., #460, SC (91604), 763-9731 QUERY LETTERS ONLY

Shapira & Assoc., David, 15301 Ventura Blvd., #345, SO (91403), 906-0322

*Shapiro-Lichtman, Inc., (P), 1800 Avenue of the Stars, #433, LA (90067), 557-2244

**Shaw Agency, Glenn, 3330 Bartham Blvd., Hwd. (90068), 851-6262

Shedd Agency, Jacqueline, 9701 Wilshire Blvd., BH (90212), 274-0978

Sherrell Agency, Lew, 7060 Hollywood Blvd., Hwd. (90028), 461-9955

Shiffrin-Barr Artists, 7466 Beverly Blvd., #205, (90036), 937-3937

**Shumaker Talent Agency, The, 10850 Riverside Dr., #410, NH (91609), . 877-3370, LETTERS ONLY

Siegal Assoc., Jerome, 8733 Sunset Blvd., LA (90069), 652-6033

Smith, Gerald K., P.O. Box 7430, Burbank, CA (91510), 849-5388

**Smith-Freedman & Assoc., 9869 Santa Monica Blvd., BH (90212), 277-8464

*Socio-Economic Research Inst. of America, Lamoree Rd., Rhinebeck, NY (12572), 914/876-3036

**Starbrite, 409 Alberto Way, #C, Los Gatos, CA (95030), 408/253-1991

Starkman Agency, The, 1501 Broadway, #301A, NY (10036), 212/921-9191

**Steele & Assoc., Ellen Lively, P.O. Box 188, Organ, NM (88052), 505/382-5863

Stone-Masser Agency, 1052 Carol Dr., LA (90069), 275-9599

**Swanson, H.N., 8523 Sunset Blvd., LA (90069), 652-5385

Talent Ent. Agency, 1607 N. El Centro Ave., #2, Hwd. (90028), 462-0913

Talent Mgmt. International, 6380 Wilshire Blvd., #910, LA (90048), 273-4000

Targ Literary Agency, Rosyln (S), 250 W. 57th St., NY (10107), 212/582-4210

*Tel-Screen Artists Int'l., 7965 SW 146th St., Miami, FL (33158), 305/235-2722

**Thompson, Willie, 3902 6th St., #213, LA (90020), 380-0676

Tobias & Assoc., Herb, 1901 Avenue of the Stars, #840, LA (90067), 277-6211

Twentieth Century Artists, 13273 Ventura Blvd., Studio City (91604), 990-8580

**Universal Artists Agency, 9465 Wilshire Blvd., #616, BH (90212), 278-2425

*Vamp Talent Agency, 713 E. La Loma Ave., #1, Somis, CA (93066), 805/485-2001

*Vass Talent Agency, 1017 N. La Cienega Blvd., #305, LA (90069), 657-1450

Videonauts Corp., Box 700-Postal Station A, 17 Front St. W, Toronto, Canada M5W 1G2, 416/929-9217

*Wain Agency, Erika, 1418 N. Highland Ave., #102, Hwd. (90028), 460-4224

Wallace & Shell Agency, (S), 177 E. 70th St., NY (10021), 212/570-9090

*Waugh Agency, Ann, 4731 Laurel Cyn. Blvd., #5, NH (91607), 980-0141

Wax & Associates, Elliot, (P), 273-8217

Webb, Ruth, 7500 Devista Dr., LA (90046), 874-1700

Weltzman & Assoc., Lew, (P), 14144 Ventura Blvd., #200, SO (91423), 995-4400

**William Jeffreys Agency, 8455 Beverly Blvd., #408, LA (90048), 651-3193

**Witzer Agency, Ted, 1900 Ave. of the Stars, #2850, LA (90067), 552-9521

World Class Talent Agency, 8530 Wilshire Blvd., #203-A, BH (90211), 655-9326

Wormser, Heldfond & Joseph, 1717 N. Highland Ave., Hwd. (90028), 466-9111

Wosk Agency, Sylvia, 439 S. La Cienega Blvd., LA (90048), 274-8063

*Wright Assoc., Ann, 8422 Melrose Pl., LA (90069), 655-5040 LETTERS ONLY

Wright Rep., Ann, 136 E. 57th St., NY (10022), 212/832-0110

Writers & Artists Agency, (P), 11726 San Vicente Blvd., #300, LA (90049), 820-2240

Writers & Artists Agency, (P), 162 W. 56th St., NY (10019), 212/246-9029

**Wunsch Agency, The, 9200 Sunset Blvd., #808, LA (90069), 278-1955

Ziegler Associates, Inc. (P), 9255 Sunset Blvd., LA (90069), 278-0070

LA—Los Angeles	NH—North Hollywood
BH—Beverly Hills	NY—New York, New York
Hwd—Hollywood	SM—Santa Monica
SC—Studio City	SF—San Francisco
SO—Sherman Oaks	

All telephone numbers are Area Code 213 unless otherwise noted.

Note: Since few agents handle Daytime writing or have any contacts in the field, a new writer would be wise to ask about this by phone or letter before sending material to any of the above.

(Reprinted with permission of the Writers Guild of America, West, Inc.)

Bibliography

BOOKS:

Adams, John R. *Harriet Beecher Stowe.* New York, Twayne Publishers, Inc., 1963.

Aristotle, Introduction to. Ed. Richard McKeon. New York, Random House, Inc. 1947.

Barnouw, Erik, *A Tower in Babel.* New York, Oxford University Press, 1966.

_____ . *The Golden Web.* New York, Oxford University Press, 1968.

Barry, Philip. *The Philadelphia Story.* New York, Samuel French, Inc., 1969.

Brady, John. *The Craft of the Screenwriter.* New York, Simon and Schuster, 1981.

Broadcasting-Cablecasting Yearbook. New York, Associated Press Broadcasting Services, 1983.

Brown, Les. *Televi\$ion: The Business Behind the Box.* New York, Harcourt Brace Jovanovich, Inc., 1971.

Cantor, Muriel G. and Suzanne Pingree. *The Soap Opera.* Beverly Hills, Sage Publications, 1983.

Edmondson, Madeleine and David Rounds. *From Mary Noble to Mary Hartan.* New York, Stein and Day, 1976.

Egri, Lajos. *The Art of Dramatic Writing.* New York, Simon and Schuster, 1960.

Ellen, Minetta. *Chatter with the Batter.* Los Angeles, Ellen, Minetta, 1948.

Forster, E.M. *Aspects of the Novel.* New York, Harcourt, Brace & Co., 1927, 1954.

Goldman, Wm. *Adventures in the Screen Trade.* New York, Warner Books, 1983.

Halberstam, David. *The Powers that Be.* New York, Alfred A. Knopf, 1979.

Hemmings, F.W.J. *Alexandre Dumas, the King of Romance.* New York, Chas. Scribner & Sons, 1979.

Higby, Mary Jane. *Tune in Tomorrow.* New York, Cowles, 1968.

Johnson, Edgar. *Charles Dickens, His Tragedy and Triumph.* New York, Simon and Schuster, Inc., 1952.

Jones, Ernest. *Hamlet and Oedipus.* New York, W.W. Norton & Co., 1976.

LaGuardia, Robert. *The Wonderful World of TV Soap Operas.* New York, Random House, Inc., 1974.

_____ . *Soap World.* New York, Arbor House, 1983.

Lemay, Harding. *Eight Years in Another World.* New York, Atheneum, 1981.

Lief, Alfred. *"It Floats," The Story of Procter & Gamble.* New York, Rinehart & Co., 1958.

McNeil, Alex. *Total Television, A Comprehensive Guide to Programming from 1948 to 1980.* New York, Penguin Books, 1980.

Murray, Gilbert. *The Classical Tradition in Poetry.* Cambridge, Mass., Harvard University Press, 1927.

Olivier, Laurence. *Confessions of an Actor, an Autobiography.* New York, Simon and Schuster, 1982.

Siepman, Charles A., *Radio's Second Chance.* Boston, Little, Brown & Co., 1946.

Soaps. Chicago, Associated Press and Norback & Co., Inc., 1983.

Scares, Manuela. *The Soap Opera Book.* New York, Crown Publishers Inc., 1978.

Stedman, Wm. *The Serials, Suspense and Drama by Installment.* Norman, Oklahoma, University of Oklahoma Press, 1977.

Wakefield, Dan. *All Her Children.* New York, Avon Books (by arrangement with Doubleday & Co.), 1977.

Warrick, Ruth with Don Preston. *The Confessions of Phoebe Tyler.* New York, Berkeley Books (by arrangement with Prentice-Hall, Inc.), 1980.

Webster's New World Companion to English and American Literature, Ed. Arthur Pollard; Assoc. Ed. for American Literature Ralph Willett. New York, Popular Library, 1976.

Writers Guild of America 1981 Theatrical and TV Basic Agreement, Los Angeles, New York, 1981.

Writers Guild of America Directory of Members, Los Angeles, New York, 1983.

PERIODICALS:

Kellogg, Mary Alice. "All the Intrigue Isn't on the Screen," *TV Guide,* Feb. 26-Mar. 4, 1983, 4.

Parker, Dorothy. "Dorothy Parker Looks at Screenwriting in 1936," *Newsletter,* Writers Guild of America, West, April, 1983.

Phillips, David P. "The Impact of Fictional Television Stories on U.S. Adult Fatalities: New Evidence on the Effect of the Mass Media on Violence." *American Journal of Sociology* Vol. 87 No. 6, May 1982, 1340-1359.

Radell, Nerissa. "Directing—the Real Power Behind Daytime," *Soap Opera Digest,* Mar. 15, 1983, 15.

_____ . "What's in the Future for 'Ryan's Hope,' " *Soap Opera Digest,* July 19, 1983, 34.

Waters, Harry, with George Hackett and Donna Foote. "Cleaning Up with the 'Sweeps,' " *Newsweek,* June 6, 1983, 85.

Waters, Harry. "The Queen of the Soaps," *Newsweek,* June 20, 1983, 76.

Willey, G.A. "End of an Era, the Daytime Radio Serials," *Journal of Broadcasting* 5, Spring, 1961, 97.

Writers Guild of America, East: *Newsletter,* Dec., 1983.

Writers Guild of America, West: *Newsletter,* Mar., 1984.

NEWSPAPERS:

Abrams, Bill. *"Fade of Soap Operas? Audiences, Sponsors Stay Tuned in Daytime,"* Wall Street Journal, July 3, 1980.

Boyer, Peter. "ABC Hopes Its Daytime Bubble Won't Burst," *Los Angeles Times,* Aug. 19, 1983.

Margulies, Lee. "CBS Wins Network Ratings Battle," *Los Angeles Times,* April 20, 1983.

_____ . "Daytime Soaps Won't Be Blacked Out," *Los Angeles Times,* April 8, 1983.

Taylor, Clarke. "The Big Apple Captures Another Soap," *Los Angeles Times,* June 24, 1983.

GLOSSARY

ad lib: a casual line not in the script.

affiliate: station contractually obligated to show an agreed-upon amount of a network's product.

AFTRA: American Federation of Television and Radio Artists.

air date: date on which a tape will be broadcast.

ASCAP: American Society of Composers, Authors and Publishers.

associate: writer hired to write scripts to headwriter's outline.

Audimeter: device for recording a household's TV-viewing habits.

backstory: events which happened before our story began.

bible: document creating a new show, including characters, locale, and two years of storylines.

blocking: working out the actors' movements.

breakdown: outline for one day's action; usually written in batches of five for a week's shows.

cable TV: method of transmission using cable instead of airwaves.

Chroma-Key: color-keyed process utilizing superimposition of foreground image against background image.

cliff-hanger: tense ending to an act or an episode.

cover sheet (or title sheet): front page of script containing episode number, tape and airdates, sets and characters.

continuity: radio or TV station department in charge of okaying material to be broadcast.

core family: central family of Daytime show about whom all action revolves.

credit crawl: rolling of credits of show's participants, run at end of show.

Crossley ratings: early system of audience sampling by phone.

C.U.: close-up.

cue cards: cards held out of camera range to cue actors in their lines.

demographics: analysis of audience by age, sex, economic status.

dissolve: cross-fade, or overlapping transition from one scene to another, usually indicating passage of time.

dream (or fantasy) sequence: brief, pretaped scene (often using an oil dissolve), to give us a look into our character's subconscious.

dry run: run-through rehearsal of a scene for cast and crew, the cast sometimes still holding their scripts.

edit: (1) polish, correct, and/or conform a script.
(2) shorten or otherwise alter (electronically) tape which has already been shot.

episode:: a single day's show.

establishing shot: a shot (usually an exterior) to tell us where we are.

fade to black: fade out.

FCC: Federal Communications Commission.

flashback: brief portion of scene from an earlier script, used as our character's "memory."

format: form in which the script is typed. (Note: in nighttime television, it means the pattern of the show itself.)

franchise character: character in position of authority, like a doctor, lawyer, judge, police officer, teacher, with "franchise" to affect other characters' lives.

headwriter: writer presently in command of the show's long- and short-term storylines. In charge of daily breakdowns and editing.

Hooper ratings: early method of audience sampling by phone call during airing of show. (Now supplanted by Nielsen ratings.)

insert: a shot, usually inanimate, of an object important to the story.

intercut: cut back and forth, as between two characters in a phone conversation.

lap dissolve: essentially the same as "dissolve," but sometimes indicating the result of previous action.

lead time: length of time between taping and airing; or between the start of the writing process and production.

limbo: small portion of a set allowing for only one character and almost no movement (phone booth, closet, hallway).

live tape: early method of taping, when lack of editing technology required a show to be produced and shot continuously, as in live production.

location: any shooting locale away from the studio.

long-range (or long-term) projection: story projection for next three, six, or twelve months.

mid-show break: long commercial break halfway through show, often including promos for the network's other programming.

mini-series: a series with a finite number of episodes.

medium shot: a shot usually including characters from about the waist up.

Nielsen rating: method of audience sampling depending on audimeters and diaries kept by viewers. (See "ratings," below.)

N/S: a nonspeaking part.

O and O: a station owned and operated by the network.

over the transom: unsolicited (as when written material is submitted without a recommendation).

pay or play: contractual arrangement specifying minimum number of days per week an actor must be guaranteed.

peak: when a storyline comes to climax.

pan: horizontal camera movement.

plotting: writing the daily breakdowns.

p.o.v. shot: point of view shot.

prime time: from eight to eleven P.M. E.S.T and P.S.T.; hours with largest number of viewers and highest costs per advertising minute.

props: properties to be used by actors on set.

ratings: audience samplings, i.e., Crossley, Hooper, Nielsen, Arbitron. (Nielsen ratings:) percentage of all sets in the country tuned to that program.

recap: recapitulation of past events.

residuals: royalty payments for reuse of material.

sample script: audition script written to a specific breakdown, but not to be aired.

send the car over the cliff: dispose summarily of a number of characters no longer needed in the storyline.

share: the share of all TV sets tuned in to a particular program.

signature: the identifying shots, graphics, logo, and theme music used for a show's opening and closing.

sponsor: the advertiser buying commercial time on a show.

Standards and Practices (sometimes combined with Continuity Dept.): Network department charged with making sure none of its programming offends public taste.

station break: a break for purposes of station (or channel) identification.

stock shot: exterior footage, usually used for an establishing shot, available from stock-shot libraries.

summary: précis of one episode's action; usually a page or two in length.

sustainer: radio show with no sponsor, sustained by station.

subtext: the emotions underlying a scene.

sweeps: the periods during year when networks attempt to boost ratings, which will in turn determine the pricing structure for advertising time.

sweetening: sound editing and adjusting, sound effects or music added after taping.

tape date: date on which episode will be taped.

t.d.: technical director

tease, teaser: opening segment(s) of show, designed to hook audience into watching.

tech: rehearsal for camera, sound, and technical effects

TelePrompTer: mechanical device (used in conjunction with the camera lens) which rolls actors' lines for prompting purposes.

throwaway line: casual line without plot significance.

tight shot: close shot.

tracking: 1. making sure a storyline is consistent from one episode to the next.
2. following a show to familiarize oneself with its story, characters and style.

trial period: first six air scripts, written before associate must be given a contract.

U/5: a part with under five lines (hence, in a separate pay category).

V.O.: Voice Over, usually indicating a character's thoughts.

VTR date: videotape recording date (tape date).

W.G.A.: Writers Guild of America.

woodshedding: rehearsing one's lines with extra care.

INDEX

Other Books of Interest

General Writing Books
   Beginning Writer's Answer Book, edited by Kirk Polking $14.95
   Getting the Words Right: How to Revise, Edit, and Rewrite, by Theodore A. Rees Cheney $13.95
   How to Become a Bestselling Author, by Stan Corwin, $14.95
   How to Get Started in Writing, by Peggy Teeters $10.95
   Knowing Where to Look: The Ultimate Guide to Research, by Lois Horowitz $16.95
   Writer's Encyclopedia, edited by Kirk Polking $19.95
   Writer's Market, $19.95
   Writer's Resource Guide, edited by Bernadine Clark $16.95
   Writing for the Joy of It, by Leonard Knott $11.95

Magazine/News Writing
   Complete Guide to Writing Nonfiction, edited by The American Society of Journalists & Authors $24.95
   Magazine Writing: The Inside Angle, by Art Spikol $12.95

Fiction Writing
   Fiction Is Folks: How to Create Unforgettable Characters, by Robert Newton Peck $11.95
   Fiction Writer's Market, edited by Jean Fredette $17.95
   Handbook of Short Story Writing, edited by Dickson and Smythe (paper) $7.95
   How to Write Best-Selling Fiction, by Dean Koontz $13.95
   Storycrafting, by Paul Darcy Boles $14.95
   Writing Romance Fiction—For Love and Money, by Helene Schellenberg Barnhart $14.95

Special Interest Writing Books
   Children's Picture Book: How to Write It, How to Sell It, by Ellen E.M. Roberts $17.95
   Complete Book of Scriptwriting, by J. Michael Straczynski $14.95
   The Craft of Lyric Writing, by Sheila Davis $16.95
   A Guide to Greeting Card Writing, edited by Larry Sandman (paper) $7.95
   How to Write a Cookbook and Get It Published, by Sara Pitzer, $15.95
   How to Write a Play, by Raymond Hull $13.95
   How to Write & Sell (Your Sense of) Humor, by Gene Perret $12.95
   How to Write "How-To" Books and Articles, by Raymond Hull (paper) $8.95
   How to Write the Story of Your Life, by Frank P. Thomas $12.95
   On Being a Poet, by Judson Jerome $14.95
   TV Scriptwriter's Handbook, by Alfred Brenner $12.95
   Travel Writer's Handbook, by Louise Zobel (paper) $8.95
   Writing for Children & Teenagers, by Lee Wyndham $11.95

The Writing Business
   Freelance Jobs for Writers, edited by Kirk Polking (paper) $7.95
   How You Can Make $20,000 a Year Writing, by Nancy Edmonds Hanson (paper) $6.95

To order directly from the publisher, include $1.50 postage and handling for 1 book and 50¢ for each additional book. Allow 30 days for delivery.

Writer's Digest Books, Dept. B, 9933 Alliance Rd., Cincinnati OH 45242
Prices subject to change without notice.